THE LAURELUDE

Books by W.N. Herbert

WN HERBERT

The Laurelude

BLOODAXE BOOKS

ISBN: 1 85224 464 X

First published 1998 by
Bloodaxe Books Ltd,
P.O. Box 1SN,
Newcastle upon Tyne NE99 1SN.

Bloodaxe Books Ltd acknowledges
the financial assistance of Northern Arts.

Cover printing by J. Thomson Colour Printers Ltd, Glasgow.

Printed in Great Britain by
Cromwell Press Ltd, Trowbridge, Wiltshire.

ACKNOWLEDGEMENTS

Acknowledgements are due to the editors of the following publications in which some of these poems first appeared: *Atlanta Review, Chapman, Comparative Criticism, Contraflow on the Super-highway, The Forward Anthology 1997, Gare Du Nord, Good Evening Mr Burns, Ibid, Janus, Lines Review, McCarapace, New Writing Scotland, Other Poetry, Poetry Review, Soho Square VII: New Scottish Writing, Verse* and *The Wide Skirt*.

Some poems have also been broadcast on BBC Radio 3, and on BBC Radio 4 on *Stanza* and *The Today Programme*.

I would like to thank Northern Arts, New Writing North, Lancaster University, Cumbria Arts in Education, and the Wordsworth Trust, for the fellowships and residencies which have supported me and my family during the writing of this book. In particular I would like to thank Claire Malcolm, Linda Anderson, Stephanie Simm and Robert Woof for all their support through some busy years.

CONTENTS

THE LAURELUDE

'Summary – Every poem is a misinterpretation of a parent poem.
A poem is not an overcoming of anxiety, but is that anxiety.
Poets' misinterpretations or poems are more drastic than critics'
misinterpretations or criticism, but there is only a difference in
degree and not at all in kind. There are no interpretations but
only misinterpretations, and so all criticism is prose poetry.'

– HAROLD BLOOM, *The Anxiety of Influence*

'I have *nothing* to say'

– OLIVER HARDY

Book One

1

One boot on Ulverston, the other stubbed
by North Shields, Stan is straddling Cumbria and
Northumberland, right hand behind him, propped
upon the Glasgow Metropole (each home
in childhood near a stage), his left hand waves
over the East Coast like a giant crow.
He's our unstable angel, bowler like
an undropped bomb. He's our colossus of
imbalance, trying to ignite the sun
with a white magic flick from his damp thumb.
Instead he makes the movies liquid, turns
Hal Roach's actors into fish, like when
the unfaithful princess in the *Arabian Nights*
transforms her husband's legs and lower parts
to black unfeeling marble, and then floods
his province so his citizens grow fins.
So Windermere fills up with Model Ts,
pianos settle on its bottom, bashed,
distorted by the slapstick fish, the shoals
of brickbats. Edgar Kennedy, the cop
whose trousers dropped, is turned into a trout,
James Finlayson's a slow burn pop-eyed pike,
Max Davidson and Charlie Chase are char
not potted yet nor panniered for the South.
Babe is a sturgeon, pregnant with roof-tacks.

2

The space between our childhood and those dreams
which charge us with restoring childhood's force
of looking and belief: that border space
is filled with film. It was a landscape, but
it flooded, and the mountains rising from
it hold strange fauna. Those who follow Jung

call this the phase of the chimerical,
a realm of creatures formed by flesh collage,
but cinema gifts us another type
of glimpse: we can see myth enacted by
special effect, by actor and cartoon.
I call the huddled witnesses to come
out from behind settees they'd like to think
protected them from yetis; those who fled
Maleficent into their mother's just
as startled arms. Can anybody doubt
that film is watched by our primeval eye
and can't be censored by the adult self
forgetting? I remember when I saw
that loud emotive gout of tartan called
Braveheart: we had to go and sink two rounds
before we'd countered the arterial flood
of righteous sentiment enough to speak
a critical word. Watching our poor past
be summoned back from playground fantasy
and the antiquarian Scots that no one read,
Blind Hary's brutal couplets (almost as
sensational as watching Mel cut throats),
I had to say 'No' to the easy wish
to claim that word claimed smooth by other mouths:
'Liberty'. Later arguments would opt
for better blades, would sharpen killing skills,
beat ploughshares into guillotines, devise
the pistol-mouth-to-nape dispersal mode
for the unrevolutionary brain,
spit millions of blood-slurry gallons that
ideological fields might receive
as fertilising – if it wasn't for
that still-mutating chemical within
the mouthful Wallace had to spill to say
it: 'Liberty'. It never stays the same
or else it always does but changes us
from governed to oppressors of our own
family, clan or nation, species, Earth.

This germ and these mutations populate
that district we have set aside to mean
all things we value but don't want to see
or carry with us through a proper day.

And so we come to walk here almost like
Greek heroes on the fields of asphodel
or US astronauts whose hopping boots
still don't quite touch the moon: displace some earth
and then we can return to actual life.
We think we've proven our take on things by
placating what we know this place should be
while secretly we'd rather hope it's not.
And so I send you, Stan, ahead of us,
squeaking and gibbering, almost putting out
your black and white St Vitus's night light:
go into the murderous page-devouring dark
and find your proper medium. Surely some
vessel can carry us across the lakes.
Beginning with Ullswater, let's attempt
negotiation with the ample night.

He gets as far as borrowing a mode
of transport from its rightful rower, then,
because he has forgotten to untie
the painter, Stan begins slowly to drag
the whole shore after his small paddle boat,
causing the hills ahead to unravel in
a compensatory stretching of the globe;
the lake to grin and spill its waters out
the corners of its moonlit mouth into
the bedrooms of the copulating poor.
Sheep lose their footing like a knitter loses
count, and fish wake in unfamiliar beds,
their local standing strangely compromised:
rowing like crazy, only Stan stays still.

3

Stan never knew the Lakes, he had no time
to cultivate that intimacy with
water that Keaton had with Tahoe, so
his next plan to complete that circuit of
the eye and the imagination which
we call the District (which is also all
anyone asks of my profession), is
as simple as an ear that's full of milk:
each night he swims them, working south to north.

Sometimes he feels a weight shift swiftly right
beneath him, just the size a man would be
but fatter, and he kicks this sense away:
one fin stroke from disruption drives us mad.
His body is the colour of old towels
dripping from one big water to the next.

At night I can attest the lakes are still
there, though it's only by the enormity
of each one's silence that you're sure of this.
And their hush differs from the hills because
you can fall in it and not find your voice,
because it's full of voices swallowed and
never returned: each drop's a locked-out word
that mixes with the unheard songs of fish,
their bubble shanties on cold silt and worms.
Whereas the hills have thinned their echoes down
till sheep and laughter and that injured 'Help!'
become a sense of constant slow approach
to their pure silence, that will not arrive.

4

Loughrigg is Stanwyck in her early films,
before her hair was struck by lightning, while
her mouth was being hardened by the flame
of Thirties' studios' cupidities –
those same fools in the forties stubbed out Stan.
The two caves are her Capra eyes, which watch
as one thing done benignly opens us
to endless harm: redemption's charmless flip.
That stupid teak-faced rich-boy dauber in
Ladies of Leisure reads her stunned relief
at being left unpawed as purity
and breaks her through to loving him or his
mistake – she ends up in a cruise ship's swell,
well, no – she lives, but everything is seen
through that night eye: the penthouse studio,
the ant-sized neon and her slinking wrap.
That mandarin laconic general,
Yen of *The Bitter Tea*, who suddenly
prefers not to shoot necessary scores
of Chinese peasantry if it upsets

this kidnapped missionary wife, and so
commits his crime against *realpolitik*
just as she understands her own desire.
Miscegenation, Barbara and montage!
I drank a glass of milk and dope and watched
thrown speechless on my parents' carpet as
she wandered through his palace ruins and
removed the cup of poison from his grip,
and squashed the long ash of his cigarette,
and placed the cushion there, behind his head
just as the faithless concubine had done
before, on the troop train, and she had watched.

Our voices echo in the flooded cave,
its slate roof gnawed by picks like toothmarks in
a cheeserind, and we hop across the stones
that lead back out: it's like a prototype
cinema, where we cluster and look out.
The sky's our stone age screen, the film is bright.
The act of opening our eyes is a
receiving of the gift of being here,
that bitter tea with no need for a cure.

5

Silver How is Harlow in the morning light.
Sometimes she just climbs in the six-inch bath
of lukewarm mist, not shivering. She turns
orange, a tint that mountains think is game.
Sometimes she pulls the mist-sheet over her
and dreams of tiny erosive feet. She can
do anything with mist, including make
silk underwear, just like the pair she wore
in *Double Whoopee* under the black gown
Stan caught in the cab door: then she parades
her self before the Prince of Wales Hotel.
Sometimes she just casts off the whole shebang
of flopped cloud into blue's wardrobe, and sits
there, glowering, ruddy, bare beneath the pale
and fading Klieg light of the morning moon.
And how appropriate that 'Silver' is,
both for the screen that Jean so quickly filled
and quickly left, and for the platinum

that was her hair's trademark, and yet her real
colour, like this hill now, was bracken red.

Could Harlow wear a kirtle? Surely she
would get away with that archaic look
this mountain does with just a skirt of trees,
hip-shrugging, corrugating, carelessly
exposing one breast's profile to our lens.
It's like there's some key scene that she's just played
which influences everyone around:
that's the way every eye keeps turning to her,
as if this change is constant but covert,
peripheral, as if her proper field
is our blind spot. If Harlow played her in
a movie it would be De Millean myth
and she would be Pandora, opener
of every box-like thing: house, heart, lake, eye.

6

Watching the mist blow over Silver How
like children on their chutes and water flumes
it's difficult to part the motion from
emotion, it's so graceful, artless, full
of what appears to be a pleasure that
the idea seeps past Caesar's bung of dust
that everything that's ever been alive
and dissipated back to atoms might
have changed or charged those particles. So plants
and creatures leak a little spirit back
to matter: that's our role, the opposite
of filtering. And all these phenomena –
the way a dry leaf scuttles on the ground
just like a crab; or how a wet leaf leaves
a perfect stain on stone, as though a text
attempts to print itself each autumn – all
suggest the world begins to feel alive:
perhaps far less than plants, or more than us.
Is that a tail-flick from the same fish seen
by Wordsworth? Had this consciousness just reached
a pitch enabling us to think it's not
that he became aware of Nature but
that it began to look at him? Well, no,

since that's the kind of fun conceit that Donne
and Marvell got to do but we can't have,
unless we prove that homeopathy's
not crap we have to put such notions in
the big placebo bag: they'll only work
if we don't know they can't. But that's the ridge
that breaks the rain-cloud's back: we know what's true
until it's been defined, at which point truth
becomes sonority, the fish is lost.

And this is just the sort of feeling caught
by tearing headlights through the nets of mist
that lie by Rydal Water in the dark:
our mind's too powerful for the shapes it makes,
it cannot catch its meanings with our hopes.

7

To drive past firs through which the sun's about
to set behind High Tove and Armboth Fell
makes branches seem light, feathery, as though
the lakeside is a wing about to lift.
The indolent blubbery rocks of Thirlmere warm
themselves like elephant seals, and I see
that solitary monster from my past:
the Edinburgh Zoo bull, perched upon
his rock as though he were its soft grey keep,
surrounded by a thin moat he would not,
as memory has it, have been able to
immerse himself in. Round this was the wall
I'd lean upon to watch him nobly snort
his prototrunk, that old boot which the Child
took to the Crocodile to ask, beside
the gravy-gray Limpopo, what it ate;
that Cumberland wish-sausage which attached
itself to the woodcutter's wife's poor nose.

Funny how everything returns to you
Stan, and to those child's tales in which you are
so easily placed, trying to remove
a lobster or perhaps some pliers from
Ollie's proboscis. It's so logical,
the formula that others' hurts heal us,

16

the audience, that every comic knows
it in their funny bone: the eye learns this,
its view distended by your simple pain.
And is this all our mogul minds will film?
those juggernauts of sentiment and greed
who never need to analyse the thing
we've always bought, that sequel to the real
picture, the one we've seen but can't recall
a detail from, just that it had you in
it and we had to laugh until we wept,
and something in the serum of those tears
keeps us afloat and paying out in pails.

8

It isn't easy for a mountain to
stand on its head: only the most graceful
will attempt it. So when all the crags that
line Thirlmere's far side upended themselves
in that clearest mirror water, I knew
rare reversals were near. It wasn't that
you couldn't tell which way up you were, but
that the precise brink vanished, making one
new shape, an amber diamond, from each hill
and its image. Looking glass stuff, as mist
poured down from Keswick way, and the sky glowed,
till lakes themselves seemed mountains on their heads
made out of water reaching into dark
earth skies, cut off from their cloud roots by air.

And then I thought of burrowing for stars:
true constellations made from the lost bones
of mother-stories; heroes from tales told
in sunken skeletons of settlements;
the texts on 3D paper, only read
on days like this, when down and up and self
and thing stand equidistant from the eye.
And then my daughter, having looked, asked for
her tape of *Alice* to be played, and we
moved north, to Penrith and the motorway.

9

It's like the slopes were giant coals that smoke
but just continually fail to light,
or they were Goths: how Siouxsie would have loved
dry ice to pour this slowly down her cheek
in one unmatched mid-eighties video.
Dinosaur hills and bishop mountains rolled
solemnly round the clunking speeding car.

Glancing right as I drove towards Penrith
past Stainton I could see beyond the hills
more hills, but caked in brilliant snow, and for
that instant, caught up by the driving, I
failed to see these were clouds, low-lying past
Ullswater, and I drove, amazed at how
different that apparent weather was –
and then I realised the daft mistake,
caused by my still not knowing all the names
and patterns of the mountains. Then I caught
myself conjecturing about that range
of cold imagined hills: what status did
it have? Was it another slab of best
chimerica? Was that an instant off–
switch for the usual mind, or could it mean
I'd got a proper glimpse into that space
where our stupid studios order what
the eye has seen into those structures which
we take as meaning real events have shapes?
I thought as I arrived to shop and swim:
perhaps I just saw other weathers and
their other hills, perhaps I just saw clouds,
but certainly the purpose of the eye
appears to be to see both worlds with one
intensity, to give the working mind
a paranoiac's problem, Dalí's take
upon the space we try to hurry through.

Book Two

'... so wide appears
The vacancy between me and those days
Which yet have such self-presence in my mind,
That musing on them, often do I seem
Two consciousnesses, conscious of myself
And of some other Being.'

                    THE PRELUDE, BOOK SECOND

1

I rise each Monday to commute and find
most times the mist's eraser has wiped out
the lake. It makes the trees across its page
appear to lose their boles, as though a herd
of Elephants' Offsprings all handed back
their trunks, defying evolution by
cocking their boot-like snoots. I climb aboard
and let those Monday mornings drive me through
the seasons, past the steam crop rising from
Rydal's brim in the first chill snap. I let
them stymie me in snow the Council thought
the weathermen were making up. I pause
upon unsalted roads to slither-stall
around slow bobsleigh hills by Windermere
with minibus and lorry and that queue
of late and reckless, terrified and numb.
The world expands back to its pre-car size,
when places were a horse's lungs apart
and distance meant something to the human foot.

The meaning of the snowdrops that begin
to echo sheep in mini herds upon
the verges flickers, Janian, and is
dependent on your sources: programmes for
the gardening sect insist they herald Spring;
whereas those mythic creatures, old wives, thought
they were death omens, not to be brought in-
doors, or, if given to a man, meant 'No'.
Ironic, given that they symbolise
the tears of Molly Bloom's precursor, she
whom Christian men have always loved to curse

for saying the first 'Yes'. These spatterings
of white upon the non-Edenic grass
could mean such other things. I let them stand
as salt-like remnants of another first:
Eve's lake of tears, as I drive past the signs
for Heaning, Mislet and Ings, thinking what
the hell's this? Hotshot lawyers of the Lakes
or sheep breed lists? M'learned ovines or
categories in Flock's *Dictionary of Fleece*?

2

Motorways make the brain drive sideways from
more safety-conscious neural routes: just so
yellow reflectors on the traffic cones
start to look like a row of daffodils.
And Harry Hamlin (that fine lawyer and
crap actor)'s early role as Perseus in
Clash of the Titans drifts to mind. How in
the Gorgon scene his brassy polished shield
prevents his further metamorphosis
from wood to brick by acting (better than
Harry) as a mirror. How this seems to mean
the movie is itself reflective, since
we see the stop-start monster but are not
transmuted: cinemas were never filled
with giggling statues, living rooms still lack
petrified children. And this role for film
was best prefigured by Cellini's boy
in the Loggia dei Lanzi with
his upheld snakeshead lantern which has yet,
with centuries of starers for its prey,
to turn a single tourist into stone.
And this affirms it is one of film's roles
to show us both the horrors that we've built
inside from bits of every injury
and animated jerkily through years
of dedicated dreaming – and the way
that looking in such mirrors may just heal.
And nothing makes this clearer than the laugh
as cut-throats, spooks and madmen all pursue
you, Stan, and queue to tie your legs around
your neck, or twist your head round like an owl.

We laugh to stop ourselves becoming stone.
We hoot because we cannot stop ourselves
becoming flesh: we've always chosen, by
our laughter, what flawed things we must become.

3

A thesis on the Orphic poets that
I've had to read at work reminds me Muir
liked to relate his adult exile from
Orkney to a general dislocation of
the islanders (and generously us)
from that fine concept: home as Eden, framed
by a child's eye (his), developed in that snap
of life it takes to have an answer to
the world's interrogation of us by
its mysteries. The answer's always our
first random action: stay and spoil it all;
or go: grow glib, as he claimed, citing that
false liberation men experience when
they work away, as I do, from their kids
and childhood, all their women's certainties.
So is it only exile, only false,
to have the time apart as I do now,
to diet, exercise and write, and is
that exile really from this deeper Muir
he marries to a place, or can that self
be simply other, rather than so lost?
My postgrad quotes from Kathleen Raine on her
view from Northumbria: Scotland as a source
of 'God's breath' coming from the border hills,
'snow clouds on the North wind'. I'm not so clear,
I can't just be impartial as the air
on this: the irony is too precise.

I'm a Dundonian, Scottish burgh-bred
and exiled to an ideal rural site
also defined as prelapsarian by
another primo vision monger while
my favourite imperfection is that town
across Raine's border, its past quickened by
such radicals as Wallace, Wedderburn,
Mealmaker, Fanny Wright and Kinloch, but

whose reputation builds its layers as slow
as Paradise's real geology.
The glaciers of its industry are gone,
the fauna of its culture felt to be
extinct by those who hurry through: no book
about Dundee thought great or read enough
to be its river's print equivalent.
Its architectural fault-lines obscure
those few poor moments when the city thought
with monuments to its recurring haze,
that comforting myopia of greed
which councils find pragmatic, meaning they
obliterate all pasts that look like slums
but build upon that civic principle:
a squalor of the mind that Orphics flee.
It's far too late for me to join them in
their dales and demi-gospels, being raised
on cow-pie and believing Bash Street School
was based upon my primary, Blackness;
opening each day television's gates
to a cartoon universe that seemed the globe's
plastic equivalent, to a monochrome
dimension where Stan danced, so *Way Out West*
he placed himself beyond our ancient edge,
those blessed islands turned to deserts where
the dead were sent to bloom: a landscape bright
and undecaying as Jerusalem
to Blake, as Scotland, Grasmere and the Bu.

Yet I knew this intense simplicity,
this place where the imagination found
whole languages of play, to be a construct;
this John the Baptist with the on-off head
to the computer Christ's new promised net
(coming soon to a decade near to yours).
It was an unreality so clear
its loveliness was lorelei-ish, but
were the gates brass and filled with bad dreams' muck?
Or horn, a cornucopia that swept
away distinctions such as true and false?

Prepared by this internalised debate,
the gauging of a scoop of earth to see
if it's more poised upon the hands of djinns,
more prior than another patch that holds
an urban sprawl, seems pretty much the same
assessment of our notions to see which
we might pretend is not a thought at all
but true, and aboriginal, and here.

4

I start by leaving Lancaster at night:
that six o' clock blackout that gradually
shifts shade, until I'm then arriving back
by Grasmere in a dusk and then a tone
for which there is no proper name, before
the gloaming, when the hit of light just starts
to soften and discolour like cut fruit.
The hills all find their hollows focussed on
like collarbones, but softly, so as not
to show their age. But I keep starting out
in January's dark: my reading has
inocculated me against that flu,
abstract thought, which our theorists of the pure
all fear, the pastoral their undeclared
model for poetry's light-thinking frame,
the lyric their – not Wordsworth's – neatest trap.
Looking right as I overtake upon
the M6 north of Carnforth I observe
at ninety miles an hour the moon emerge
from a huge boscage of black cloud and blind
the plain of air we race below with milk.
Turning at February off onto
the Kendal road I find the loudest tapes
that kick my students' jamming signals out,
the ones that April makes into a sound-
track for the loll of hill and slew of lake,
the deafening new leaves, the feedback from
the lambs. But on the 591 in March
I'm still aware of darkness: how the cars
desert you sometimes for a minute at
a time, no headlights' whites ahead, no reds,

your mirror emptied and the road devoid
of strong restriction. This is how it was
in Kansas as *Père Ubu* now divulge:
in 1904 the only two cars in
that flat state smashed each other. If I hit
anything now it would be a Model T
driven by the drowned corpse of Oliver.

By May I'm thinking back to last year: Dad
in Letterkenny leaking black into
the toilet pan, the tests gone through him like
a grope of that same lightning – that same bolt
that pulled Babe Hardy down, punched Harlow in
the liver and destroyed the infants of
those terrifying poems, 'Surprised by joy'
and *Epitaph*. My father always was
Barnacle Bill himself, big-bellied as
the merchant ships he sailed around the world
three times in those same Fifties Laurel kissed
goodbye to Hardy. Dad was then a thin
and rakish engineer: I grew up on
his tales piled high as spinach tins, as full
of iron as he now lay drained and white
without a wrinkle in the Mater in
Eccles Street, where Bloom took Stan Dedalus
for cocoa.* As the operation nears
I'm flying there still, looking at the Joyce
Aer Lingus scribble on seat covers as
I drive towards Loughrigg. That mountain frames
my mirror so the road behind appears
to plough right up the stomach of the hill.
Mister O'Malley can't quite bring himself
to spell things out for me, his hands don't know,
cavernous haemangeoma just won't scan:
it's like a small medusa, Mum is told,
as though that's like an image we can see.
I have a haircut for my birthday in
the salon just beside the guest house, and

---

* 'At the housesteps of the 4th of the equidifferent uneven numbers,
number 7 Eccles street, he inserted his hand mechanically into the back
pocket of his trousers to obtain his latchkey.' – JAMES JOYCE, *Ulysses*

the girl decides my first name's Herbert, and
I lie in bed below a virgin and
child done by a Bible-thumping Chinese nun,
and the effect is strangely Daoist, like
the way that driving late at night reminds
you that the soul has a direction, that
you're pointed at a place and down a route
as plain as road-maps dream of being, chucked
behind you, drowsing on the seat. Perhaps
this is the mark that Stan's been thrown towards,
I think as I speed past the bluebell woods
that work won't let me walk in and pull up
in June, the heat uncurling fiddle-heads
and shoving mouthfuls of dry petals out
of poppies' hairy buds like paper from
a cunt in just that evening light we know.
I carry crates of stories in and see
if Dad has left a message on the phone.

Book Three

*'...might we not venture that the birth of the reader is not
achieved at the cost of the death of the author, but rather
at that of showing how the critic too becomes an author.'*

SEÁN BURKE, The Death and Return of the Author

1

I watch Stan start to scramble up Loughrigg
as if he's following some preset way,
a pattern of migration cuckoos know,
and there's a nest somewhere he must usurp.

That's how he first appeared to me, full-grown,
and travelling his non-roads north, as though
he's not my own idea. All I see
is him, alone, which makes me wonder: why
did I bereave him? And when are you, Stan?
I know you're going on to struggle up
the mountains with the silliest names in search
of comic Pisgah, somewhere Ollie might
be visible from – Dowp, Great Cockup, Barf,
Middle Tongue, Near Swine Crag and Starling Dodd –
but when are you in real time? By his bed
after the stroke, or back in your hotel
in the long silent doze before your line:
'I wish that I was skiing.' 'Do you ski
then, Mister Laurel?' 'No, but anything's
better than lying here while you stick all
these needles in me.' Is it even you
who's telling this? Is Hardy, like the man
who wrote a novel with an eyelid's twitch,
or like the Red King, dreaming you and me?
Or are you now that other Hardy who
before you started filming found his loss
more powerful than presence, writing for
his first wife's sunken ghost a poetry
that neither she nor her successor would
be subject to alive? You make me think
you filmed those widowed scripts inside your head,

the shows you'd written by the time he died,
rehearsed and played them all, refining gags
that no one else could see, in just the way
you do not ski round Cumbria, but climb
upon the icy bellies of the hills,
those bergs that sank the ship-shaped lakes and left
their islands sticking out like funnel stacks,
as though the District was a string of Pearl
Harbours, a rusting trench of Scapa Flows.

2

It's not a cottage nor an industry,
it's more a college or a set of cells:
a Celtic monastery without much rule,
but beehive-like, the workers toiling for
a dead man's muse, though most of these monks think
that the museum is their proper queen.
Madonna of the Documents, they pray,
Mary of Paintings, Prints and Catalogues,
do not let us stray into verse, but keep
the tourists coming, may the Japanese
bring their chrysanthemum-like wads of cash
to blossom here, and let the Yanks still lay
their offertory flashes at our door.
And like that dance of dons before the text
they're waiting for advancement to real jobs:
Curator of the Creetown Gallery
of semi-precious stones; Chief Archivist
of porcelain doll limbs (Victorian);
Publicist for the foremost litter-tray
producer in Northants. It makes the few
who tend the actual honey look like drones;
it makes their faith comedic, shambling, full –
for if this is a tumour it's benign,
a subsequent growth like shiitake on
an ageing limb, and what has burgeoned here's
our true response to poetry: preserve
and package, sanctify, resent and gape,
envy, dismiss, obsess, don't buy, and here
and there, because of all this work, just read.

Can living here be simpler than my task?
where every sense is educated by
the past — its walkers, starers, scholars — can
anyone here achieve a single glance
not filtered through the eyes of Wordsworth or
Wainwright? A writer has some strategies
for seeing in comparison, and can
impersonate the Chinese poet in
the habitat of his immortals, where
humility breeds variation on
the perfect, ancient and completed themes.
He knows to borrow that barbarian touch
that readers might feel just rejuvenates
but these old masters wouldn't recognise
as art. The Beijing poet Yang Lian
has only now alliterated for
the first time in four thousand years of verse.
Last time we talked, and drank that rocket fuel
which he prefers to malt, he mentioned forms
I'd thought made up by the surrealists:
alternate lines of verse and prose; a voice
that treats the narrative-inducing self
as though it were a character; the prose
that rhymes the Euphemists could not achieve
in English — each with their millennia
of craft behind it — and the closest one
to my beginnings of concerns was *t'zu*,
the poem filling up the perfect mould
of characters a previous song had left,
matching it syllable for syllable
like an impersonator who appears
to ape a star or politician but
starts throwing out strong changes on their themes
and wildest is best.* I could read in these
that portly outline on my inner screen,
the mirror of Stan's absent partner: Bloom.

---

* 'When the poet selected an existing tune he was bound by its whole
structure. The tunes registered in the catalogue under the title of the
original song determined not only the total number of words (i.e.
characters and therefore syllables) in any given poem, but also the
division into stanzas (tuan) and the lengths of the lines...'
— J.PRUSEK, from the definition of T'zu, *Dictionary of Oriental Literature*

3

Poets get haunted by the critics as
anyone is by ghosts: not really, but
never quite not at all. They seem to want
that value they think they alone attach
to us like phantom medals, pinning us
down and through, a value no one else, perhaps
especially us, ever fully feels.
And so we are declared heroic and
extinct at the same time, by those who hope
to usurp their own invention, that weed square
and tar-burst former airfield, which we know
was never used for war. In fact it's just
some grass where, these days, the Grasmere Games are held.
But watch the newsreel of the way they marched
(since critics, like ghosts, occupy our past,
perhaps I'd better put them in that tense),
flickering in black and white across their fields
of research: if you can see them at all,

watch Hugh Blair's Light Belle-Lettreistes, Arnold's Own,
The Leavis Watch, Urn's Regiment (Well-Wrought);
and then the foreign legions: Barthes' Hussars
and Derrida's Guerrillas, Debord's squad
of kamikaze Situationists,
then Bakhtin's Signal Corp. Their systems more
advanced than any reader, they prepared
their most audacious blitzkrieg. Having killed
the dodo author (though Sean Burke has claimed
that creature can be traced – and uses those
same instruments deployed in its demise),
they then wished to invade the reader's role,
that gentle space, dictate not only how
the thing that's being read must be defined,
but how the act of reading should take place.
Having knocked off their Roland in the joust
to which, thus proven dead, he could not be
invited, next they'd put the riderless
horse of text through such feats of dressage no
now-displaced reader would feel fit to judge.
So could you all please leave their splendid park,
your former common. As I trespass there

upon that other moor where others say
we used to meet (a claim I somehow doubt:
I know the poets used 'real language' – theirs –
but did the readers' silence listen or
was it just rage at our ventriloquy?)
I feel one shadow always drawing close.

In life a rounded man, defender of
our letters, stitcher-up of canons and
the diagnosing surgeon of all text,
whose corpus he found critical but still
delectable as it lay dying in
his nurturing hands. This could be delayed:
simple misprision of the symptoms would
create a lingering death-in-life for books
in which their paper sickness would become
for stronger sufferers, unique good health,
a self-delusion only he, of course,
could minister, but still remission from
the general end of all our literature.
And so his rows of lucky princes sit
in lotus pose, turned marble to their necks.
His name was Bloom, and like his Dublin twin,
his actions were the shadow of a myth,
though he knew he was his creator's tool.
His myth was entropy, the Word of God
shattering through creation's need for time,
its echoes always less and less until
they would return to universal hush.
Bloom too roams through a city made of words
in search of every splinter, every phrase
which might contain a variation on
the original sound. So I feel him here,
library-chaser, ghoul of manuscripts,
drawn to the District by the scent of ink.

4

It's marvellous the way that bowler sticks
above Stan's brows despite his douking in
the lakes and those high winds among the crags:
he's like a little chess piece stomping on
to his determined final move, that square

30

he can't pin down, that's like a sheet pegged out
before him, always just receding from
his touch. It shows him movies from those lives
that echo his: see Valéry, as Stan
slips down the scree, draft M. Teste's attempt
to focus only on his hands and feet,
to scramble and stay sane in *Idée Fixe*.
And there is Valda Grieve collecting eggs
to feed MacDiarmid from the Whalsay cliffs
before he goes quite mad from the neglect.
Here's me upon the beach beyond Arbroath,
climbing the red-faced sandstone to ignore
Nancy's attentions after my break-up
with Helen. How I couldn't handle her
just then, that confident Bostonian
sexual push drove me up the sea-cliff past
the safe-to-fall point, where the gulls began
resenting my hand-holds. The plate glass-edged
horizon pressed upon my nape – and there
before me in that random spot I'd reached
were carved initials that matched mine, a curved
'W.H.', quite eighteenth-century,
that nearly made me fall on her, hunched, bored
beneath me in her turtle-shit green smock.

I have to stop him there, his arms filled with
Lent lilies, Tenby daffs, the latter rare
as they were common back when Dorothy
first saw them, back when William borrowed words
(first hers, then Mary's) to make poetry
out of the simply seen: always an act
of theft or dubious alchemy. How does
it go? Stan, you should know this much at least:

> 'I wandered lonely as a trout
> that doesn't like to swim in shoals
> when all at once I heard a shout
> from little prawns that lay on coals
> upon the barbies by the lake,
> sputtering and charring flesh to flake.

'Harmonious as the stars that shriek
and whirl around their nightly wheel
they yelled in French and broken Greek,
and after this al fresco meal
ten thousand tourists swilled in rills,
flossing their teeth with daffodils.'

Prolonged immersion in the Lakes would seem
to induce decomposition of the text:
this flying trout is not indigenous,
its message slightly pickled, even smoked.
Its flesh's grain is darker, wilder, less
upbeat. Perhaps if you continued things
would seem more Spring-like, unified with all
the crucial elements of usual verse?

'The fishes in the friendly mere
suggested that I should return
to an element devoid of fear
where no one's ever seen to burn:
all company, I disagreed,
contains the pain of thoughtless greed.

'And even flowers suck the sun
that sinks down emptied every night
just as I flop and try to shun
the vision of each victim's fright.
Small wonder, then, I go without
and wander lonely as a trout.'

Perhaps not. Let me see that volume which
you carry under your lyrical hat:
The Solitary Weeper – that suits you –
'The squirrel's too much with us, take his spoon'?
We are Statistics of Mortality?
What are *The Brucie Poems?* songs on golf?
'Beloved pail I sit upon', now that's
Oor Wullie, surely: a dungareed wee blond,
Dundee's spike-headed cartoon mascot, not
the proper sort of William, not at all.
These others have become too rude to read:
'The child is lathering his spam', *The Porn*.
The only one unaltered by your stint
beneath the brim's, of course, *The Idiot Boy*.

5

All poetry is theory or the state
to which (hush hush) all theory aspires.
Theory defeated poetry, usurped
its role before my generation had
begun to write, because the self is far
too large a concept for the current soul
to fill: it can't abide the vacuum left
by Rousseau for our bigger thoughts, and so
it papers over oceans with a chart
which Freud supposed we'd fill with unknown things,
which Jung suspected we'd already done.
Remember the zen master who was asked
what should we do about our dreams? He said
'Forget them.'
        Wordsworth, then MacDiarmid thought
that science was the necessary lump
of ballast for an epic ship, but most
day-trippers say, 'Forget that too.' The world
is not composed of pilgrims, voyagers
or saints: the Heyerdahls and Jumblies now
sail on our duplex screens and not our seas.
Nor can the deeps conceptual space appears
to offer Hawking, Feynman, Gould, attempt
to rival *Star Trek*'s grip on future things.
Design will always drown technology
out: not to notice this would sink our books
quicker than Cyclops chucking islands at
a sieve. We seem to have no subject, just
the susurrations of the words, but these
can never stop impersonating states
of mind we care about: this is our port
of call and destination, this is all
our cargo, map and compass, crew and mast.

Does anyone watch these self-creating storms?
Wait at their terminal for spirit news
or listen on their cellular to how
we're perishing for want of privilege?
It hardly matters when it's not our mission
to explore old tropes and find the slant that fills
the sail, that seems enough to boldly school
new readers in our ancient folly: we

pack out the mind with language that confronts
its need to be bone-bright to thole its end.

6

Ten thousand things are chocking in like flakes
on polar balaclavas, florets on
a cauliflower – as my daughter called
the morning's snow she'd squeezed into a clutch.
I think of freezing women, drowning men:
mothers and brothers. Izzie gathers moss
in John's Grove to make 'tea'; Stan Laurel drinks
an entire water barrel; Hardy stands
on a dark doorstep, nightshirt hung with frost.
The snow is dark flecks when you look up at
the clouds it's falling from, and somewhere there's
a *Book of Snowflakes* photographed to prove
they have no twins, and somewhere there's a flake
that's falling that's identical to one
inside the snowball Izzie made out there
between the places Dorothy would walk
between them: William and John, each drop lost
eventually in their various seas.

This saturation of the land with names
is something I can only slowly grasp:
that here is where that poem should be placed
and not the set my mind knocked up for it.
We've always overlain them with ourselves,
so Izzie's playing in that drowning grove
where both of them lay in a ditch and thought
how good it would be to be dead and hear
a silence that is broken now by cars
and voices from a class they couldn't know
would soon proliferate far worse than sheep,
replacing industry with a proud drawl
they think will mimic total ownership.

I'm reading *Lucy Gray* again and still
can't manage it without a laugh, whereas
the poem on his daughter makes me sob
like certain songs – we've all got ten or so
we use as talismans against the worst.

34

Those nights my daughter's temperature goes for
a fire-walk I lie there and listen to
the water timer click, that distant owl,
the one same solitary car roll past
over and over and I think of how
his children left him for their little graves.
All speculations on the hour end here:
it's far too early, soon enough for sleep
which will not come till she wakes up as well
as drugs they didn't have can now predict.
And what about those other drugs I took
ten years too much of to consider now
poor Coleridge without that partial wince
of recognition at his perfect sloth,
that clarified inertia of the stoned?

It's weird how spores of comedy invade
all others' tragedies for us, and how
that laugh can save us briefly from our own.
The laugh, like ghosts, or like those words they call
symbolic forms (because they stand between
the non-echoic – 'bed' – and terms like 'snore'
or 'rumpy-pumpy' – and just seem to point
at meanings: 'gleg' and 'glaur' and maybe 'gasp'),
the laugh can feed our faith unlikely things
make sense, that luck and other clues, remains
of systems, incoherencies and signs
show chaos can enfold us, be complete,
maternal in the fleshless face of law,
its pact between mathematics and the stars.
Dark matter is all round our orderings,
it holds us in a way we recognise
is fathomless and terrible as love.

Book Four

1

Stan leaps abruptly up Helm Crag, and stands
between the Lion and the Lamb. His suit
has somehow reappeared upon him when
we go to zoom. He's formal as a don,
Carrollian, a Herald – one of those
last-century inventions that chess dismissed –
and now he's gone from sight, to Gibson Knott,
and over by Ullscarf to Borrowdale.
I'm left to recognise this place has traits
of desolation, from the watercress
in Rothay, which was meant to cure the mad,
to the Lamb, also known as the Organist,
a Batesian old lady who appears
to a paranoiac eye not only to
be watching but to knit as she shifts shape:
one plain one ewe one purl one spinster, quite
titanic. Now the whole vale should close in,
demanding that I find it peaceful and
profoundly still, past speaking of and to.
A year here's quite enough for folk like that,
the sheep-shape claims, now writing, as the wait
for summer shows on days like this, when light
refuses to admit abstraction. But
patches of sun, hill-windows open on
this quiddity of green that she describes,
squid-herds of pale ink clouds pass over and
the hills become moles, huge in velvets, or
the horns of deer in close-up, almost limbs
and backs of some amorphous *Star Wars* blobs
for whom, the ewe would claim, I constitute
their only, aberrant narrator here.

And now that light consents to dim enough
to smooth out voices from the rubble-top
and let an epic text commence its scroll
across the heavens as our film begins:

'A century can usually expect
to outlive the souls it shares a birthday with:
their childhood massacres (one's of those near-
immortals, toys; the other's of all flesh
that threatens) stem from hates they've been bequeathed.
Their youthful shifts in seeing shake them both
more deeply than perspective will dictate,
but one's arrival at this station marks
the drift: two middle ages now begin.
One faces compromise's kisses whilst
their twin's still filled with anger and mistakes
that stem from its dream of authority.
The flesh of one flares in a quick-fit purge
designed to save the same shot thinking which
their role in starting's now beyond debate.
The final thirty years just stumbles on,
lacks distance to escape the smoking view.'

After the film's begun the rest of us
arrive and try to find our places in
a dark our predecessors can't now see,
and our debates, our whispering critiques,
are those of the disjunctive singleton
I find myself becoming as I age.
I never was the soul I aimed myself
so surely at becoming, ending up
another version of my actual dates:
the late and cooling decades which can't see
the next tyrannical child, strong enough
to strangle snakes, steal cattle or invent
an instrument that sweeps our labours out
with one strum – turtle-turning all those hopes.

Perhaps that's why I so identify
with over-shadowed selves: the way that Stan
seems led by Hardy, or how Coleridge
appeared to fail. My vote is always for
Dizzy as well as Bird, for Beefheart and
for Zappa, Clift as well as Brando: for
'as well', for 'other', and for 'more', for in
that augmentation I can feel the shape
that I, my culture and my language, can
begin to occupy, at arm's length from,
on tongue's tip, in the background to

that thing disqualified from being real
by standing in the complex net of years
and simply saying so – in short, the star,
the steadfast mouth, the lout, Wordsworthian,
the striding truth with Charlton Heston teeth
and the moustache of Stalin hovering by
like a soft bat, a vulture made of hair.

The fear of definitions drives me back
indoors, to dictionaries' deferrals and
the videos that flock about my set.
No news is poetry that stays news good
enough to watch and watch instead of read
the thousand books that crouch out in the lane
and know I'm wrong, though their Olivier tones
cut through the scores by Hatley, themes by Shield.
If I had any wagons I'd get in
a circle. As the actress may have said
to Stanley, 'I've got you surrounded, kid.'

2

Dead relatives have moved in to the house
next door. They pass me in the midnight lane
and say, 'You're taller.' They present their mouths
for beetroot-and-leukaemia kisses. They
know all about our bedroom problems but
are far too bored to mention them. They think
another woman would give me a son.
They tempt me by agreeing with my shames.
They're worried my anxiety will drive
me mad. Their big pursed lips are pressed
to every window. They say, 'Don't you think
it's odd your parents are called Dorothy
and William?' but they won't tell me the things
about themselves that helped me be this scared.
They won't explain this silence that they fill.

Loneliness is a sign of presence in
the place of the dead: they do not reply
in a particular pitch that explains their case.
There's knowing everything, and things it is
appropriate to lose when others die.

They should be able to take with them, not
secrets but just grave goods: the beaker filled
with oats; the photos with lost faces; names
we do not know the history behind;
gone footage; confrontations that did not
fit in the journal; days the sun just froze
and wouldn't give their childhood, children, sweet-
heart, conscience, inspiration, health or hope –
just wouldn't give it back. These things they keep.

3

Stan has been trapped at Borrowdale behind
the wall they built to keep their cuckoo in
and so preserve one Spring forever: it's
disrupting how my poem's seasons roll,
the way a piece of film can cut up time,
or metre substitutes its intervals
for our durations.* That is why he's stuck
before a stack of dry stone ictuses:
he knows a camera when it points at him.
And that's why I keep waking on the wrong
birthday: it's always Wordsworth's and not Stan's.
I stand in our museum and recite
the *Intimations* and *Dejection* yet
again, then go to Tweedies and get drunk.
Alberz's run repeats itself, his cross
cuts back across the goal: I watch McCoist
arriving, horizontal, from the same
nowhere, to nut the same ball home, and know
this being Auld Firm, that in Donegal
my father will be groaning in Jack's Bar,
and thinking (wrongly) that the jammy fuck's
got in the Scotland squad at thirty five.
Then tottering in late afternoon again
to see how all the graves are getting on.

* 'Spring being very charming in Borrowdale, and the sound of the cuckoo
gladsome, the people determined to build a wall to keep in the cuckoo, and
make the Spring last forever. So they built a wall across the entrance at Grange.
The plan did not answer; but that was, according to the popular belief from
generation to generation, because the wall was not built one course higher.'
– DAVID RAMSHAW, *The English Lakes*

Note: Wordsworth's birthday is on April 7, Stan Laurel's on Bloomsday, June 16.

4

We're always touched by accidental shapes:
those ceremonies rising from events
you never thought of as significant.
So when my day-job got me chaunting both
that ode and Coleridge's like two parts
of one heartbeat – the birth day's festival –
I didn't at once notice how my own
days had begun to match that pulse: between
the home I'm rarely at as sanctuary
of sorts, and here as dawning of the fear
of loss of the ability to love,
until I sat down drunk in Grasmere church-
yard and watched rain deciphering the stones
into the breasts of all the birds around
singing their inconsolable laments
on being unintelligible, on
being the messengers of God, their text
fully translated into greed and lust,
anxiety, and fear of making sense.
I saw his grave's expression ran from calm
to distant disapproval, knew my stance
as perfectly as birds are understood.
I read his son and daughter's stones again
and didn't envy him as Coleridge did
his placedness: he couldn't hope to grow
from these two roots. I wasn't tempted by
belonging here exactly as I've stopped
believing in the further lover or
the second child. Translating how things are
into the way we think about them brings
us close enough to clarity of grief
to know that we have business to complete.

5

You can't rewind the video of your brain
exactly though all memory appears
as interactive, so I don't know which
came first: the image of his bowler flung
like Oddjob's to a boat on Derwent, or
the memory of Penrith in New Year snow.

We came down from Dundee in thickening blasts
that slowly choked the road out like a thumb:
its swirling print began to press for real
on Crawfordjohn's carotid: watching from
the *Little Chef* we dreamt we might get through
before it whited out, slid on until
the emperor penguin beak-to-tailing cars
began to climb the weak lines of that track
the motorway had dwindled to by Shap.
Abruptly we saw policemen loom with lights
that blinked once in our wipers then we found
that we were pointed in the opposite
direction, north from all that emptying
of owls and pillows to Penrith and to
the George Hotel.

              Once through the swivel doors
I knew this for a massing of my past:
milk porcelain pastoraulers over fires;
teak cabinets that writhed on stubby legs;
wallpaper, thick, embossed, and painted cream;
carpets with jugged hare patterns, floors that lurched
as though the ship was heaving; armchairs deep
as setts, from which you pressed a bell for tea
from notched and scorching silver and for toast
so buttered that your hand crept to your heart.
We sat and steamed in this amalgam of
my Aunty Bella's and the Airlie Arms:
Brechin and Kirriemuir – the family and
the public spaces merging in small towns.
Everybody came here in the flow
of hours, the matriarchs, the couples, kids:
we watched this accent go about its days
until the snow began to lift, and I
sat in the window thinking we should go
and watched the people shop in Arnison's
for corsets, camisoles and diamond socks.

This was the first place in this country that
I'd felt at all like mine, and yet it was
the vanished parts – those childhood zones – it matched
as though these were those dead regained. At that
I found that I was looking at one thing –

not a diversity with people in,
but just a static entity made up
of spaces in between the buildings – and
the buildings; of the movements of these folk
as much as these folk moving – all that froze
as though the people were each envelopes
containing a large letter from one thing
still being said I couldn't quite make out:
we thought that we were individual
because that's just the way the letter fits.
Then it was time to pack and go back south.

The other image I made up, of course:
how William Brownrigg caught the hat and found
that it was full of virgin olive oil,
how he and Franklin rowed out past the isle
where Herbert lived, and spooned a little out
pouring it carefully upon the chop
of waters, watching as it spread out in
a halo till, one molecule thick, it
calmed everything down to its usual pace.*

6

I'll leave the bigger hills for Coleridge,
his brockenspecter striding over from
Helvellyn carrying the uncarved block
of his achievement: knowing what to write
too well to write it. Wordsworth knew enough
to get it done by being wrong about
the right things: where we are before we're born
and why we think we're being spoken to
by rocks and stars. I'll sprawl upon a hill
as intimate as White Moss, watch the cars
crawl round the banks of Rydal, follow jet
roars, listen for goose clunks, occasional

* '…Benjamin Franklin stayed [at Ormathwaite in 1772], preoccupied, quite
literally, with the problem of pouring oil on troubled waters. He, Brownrigg and
the Rev. Charles Farrish of Carlisle carried out experiments on Derwentwater,
and one wonders if anyone protested when the three of them rowed out from
Friar's Crag and tipped barrels of oil onto the choppy waters of the lake.'
– NORMAN NICHOLSON, The Lakers

raven falsettos, lambs that bawl out 'Yeah!',
and let the chaff of bugs blow by, birds tune
in and out, grass ears wave, the heather-like
white blossoms dot between the rock chunks,
the lichens pale and lime and charred. To sit
this high and see enough and be contained
by all these barer hills declares the truce
between adrenaline and soul that gives
you somewhere in the psyche to subsist.

Descending through the ferns into John's Grove
the little white stuff like cowparsley looks
like starmaps (Pamela called it saxifrage),
and moss is clustered on the tree-trunks like
the shadow heads of ancestors thrown on
the vanished Dundee screens: the Tivoli,
the Regent, the Palladium, the Rex.
I know it's clover all behind the bench
but not which trees these are that nod, horse-like,
as I look at the little island with
bare branches on it like the bones of whales
and listen to – nuthatches, maybe a wren?
These nameless plants and songs that others know
like Adam: I don't speak these dialects
of chlorophyll and feather, feel before
that moment of identity. I go
home past the row of rhododendrons as
the rain approaches, hearing late bees fill
their scentless purples with a traffic buzz.

7

Sometimes I come down in the vodka light
of one or two a.m. and watch the moon
sit in Dove Cottage like a cuckoo's egg,
considering the poem that it's scared
to print, those backward scribbles hidden in
the dust of darkside craters, whose new names
are still a fankle to wear well, and think
about the Southern constellations: how
their first names and their old shapes broke apart,
dissolved before the focus of new eyes –
Bayer, Lacaille, de Houtman, Keyser, Todd.

My brains feel like a jumbled tape that's built
new darkness from a print-filled memory.
De Quincy plays the Cuckoo Opening
each rigid midnight with René Magritte
while Loulou's burning Pomeranian doup
chars the land's floorboards. Walter Scott hands out
deformed wee terriers like visiting cards,
and William and his sister clutch their jaws,
their skulls, their stomachs in an agony
of owning their imaginations, of
hearing Eden, contrariwise to clocks
and locomotion, to electric looms
and hand-held organisers, helpless as
Laurel, strange legionnaire, Quixotic chump,
to deal with gas pills, wind-up gramophones,
or how their logic's lost by being saved
in our analysis, the way we lose
a lover by preserving lust, a child
by never touching their divergent pulse.
Only that inner chaos, failing to
consume correctly, its capacity
for error pushed by love, can still hold them:
our small responsive chaos holds them all.

The posture of the lamppost opposite
betrays Stan's presence, never mind the dead
giveaway of its bowler halo, so
I slump beneath the bats and watch those bright
principles, pole and sphere, confuse me with
simplicity: the funny thing that is
not happening, but is, is being, is.

8

When I crawl back he's ready to depart.
He does a sand dance on my kitchen floor,
those chill slate flags; he mugs, and toodle pips.
He's wrapped a toga-towel about him like
an am-dram Roman, like his name's old source:
that plate of Scipio in his laurels in
the book Stan's first wife opened randomly.
A Sortes Africanus Jung would like

with his belief in synchronicity,
his dream of Africa as otherwhere,
so maybe that's the note to let him loose.

Underwhelmed by the charms of Europe, Jung
broke out of its elaborate nets, wrote,
'This Africa's incredible! The soil
is towering up the noble, spreading shapes
of the great Atlas range – and Sousse's ships!
I've painted that lateen-sailed one before.
I do not know what Africa is saying:
you stumble over Roman pottery,
amphorae from antiquity just sit
in the bazaar, then there's the moon!' He spent
hours in the coffee-houses, listening
and understanding nothing. 'You're so large
that you could lift the sky,' was what they said.
'What Europeans see as apathy,
a mask, I sense is agitation, but
I can't explain it. Why does Moorish earth
so smell of blood? Rome, Carthage, Christ: the blood
exceeds its ages.' Pressing on to Sfax
he entered the Sahara's dreams, and came
to the oasis city of Tozeur.
'Processions of alfalfa, apricot
and peach trees – green, gold, white – a Paradise
in which the kingfishers are angels and
a spirit's breaking through the crust in springs.'
And in the shade of date palms he soon found
most of the white-clad figures to be men.
He wrote, 'They hold each other in a close
embrace, my dragoman confirms this.' Soon
departing, glancing at his pocket watch.
But on the roadless sift to Nefta Jung
discovered one who, 'mounted on a mule
studded with silver, passed without a word,
without a note of that faint foolishness
which clings to Europeans'. There he found
a marabout was rushing into town
with drums and the dramatic great green flag
which signalled all the ghost-dust tribesman to
the digging of an irrigation ditch.

He distanced from the hoes and baskets that,
frenzying at the ground to drumbeats, tore
a tongue of dry earth out in two days, whilst,
utterly white, the marabout controlled
this dance. The workers dropped asleep beside
the trench, and when 'the invitation to
the muezzin coincided with the dawn,
I left. Infected psychically, next day
I'd enteritis and I hurriedly
returned to Tunis'. But before he sailed
back to Marseilles and all those myths, he dreamt
he stood upon a wooden bridge into
a casbah in the middle of a plain.
Halfway across, that Arab, burnoused in
a white thing like a towel, silently
emerged, and grappled with him. Being large,
he took the clash, and both plunged in the moat.
That prince then 'pushed my head beneath the green'.
When he reciprocated, not to kill
but only to control, he found they both
were transferred to an octagonal room in
the inner citadel, with low divans
and marble walls. The ghost was looking at
a book: 'magnificent calligraphy
on milk-white parchment', which he felt was his
although he didn't know its contents. This
enormous book they then sat down and read.

OTHERMOOR

'…it is a privilege to see so
much confusion…'

— MARIANNE MOORE

The Cutting Up of the UK

> 'She was so little acquainted with the geography of the
> island, that she imagined we could not go to Scotland but
> by sea; and, after we passed through the town of Berwick,
> when [Mr Bramble] told her we were on Scottish ground,
> she could scarcely believe the assertion.'
>
> TOBIAS SMOLLETT, Humphrey Clinker

When did your country end:
the moment mine began?
When a tectonic seizure
origamied our north to yours,
we confused, becoming Othermoor.
The cities ground together
in wheezy concrete harmonies:
Leithchester and Aberleeds,
Duncastle, Livergow.
When Criffel piled on Skiddaw
but the Grampians plunged
the Pennines in an anti-range,
a thousand-metre trench
called Mistress Bramble's Minch.
Severed from Middlebrum
and the Mouth, our kingdom
was a shrunken headland, compressed
by fathoms of history, a place
where a back-door duke can visit
every woman in one night
as long as his slipper's vitreous
enough for entry. Where the virtuous
ask forgiveness of the stars
for not kissing their lucky arses.
Where every village, each street
is falling on their feet.

An Address to the English

Eh'm staunin here feelin a wee bit crabby
cause thi anely rhyme Eh can find fur 'Rabbie'
is thi bluidy awful standirt habbie
      that wiz his stanza,
which – if ye treh ut – aye soonds flabby
      and you a chancer.

Eh'm also cursin wan Seán Burke
fur breedin me a hangover, thi jerk,
jist when Eh hud tae write this wark
      ma heid wiz a sponge
that hud sooked a Tyne and Wear o murk:
      a reid blancmange.

Whit are we daein here, by Gweed,
you hearin me spoot oot a leid
ye haurdly follae and damn few read
      withooten tears,
tae celebrate some boozer deid
      twa hunnert years?

His morals werenae aa that PC,
his sentiment a wee thing cheesy,
his hairstyle wiz a quiffy greasy,
      auld Elvis Burns –
but still, he gote me oan BBC:
      that's a stunt that earns.

His gender views were somethin brassy
his Suppers toast thi female chassis
thi semm wad turn meh wife's fiss glassy
      gin ut reached hur lug –
Eh'll hae tae raise ma gless tae Lassie
      that filmic dug.

His politics were kinna muddy:
a tory when tipped thi noble noddy
syne nationalist and unca bloody
      fehv meenuts later –
whit're we daein cheerin a shoddy
      auld fornicator?

But mebbe you're a better lot
tae celebrate'um than some Scot
wha's curled up drunk in a parritch pot
      and gone tae sleep –
whit's great in Burns rewrites thi plot
      Scots maistly keep.

Thi thing is, since you cannae dae
thi accent, then ye dinnae play
oor sad auld kiddy-oan we'd say
      thi semm wirsel,
gin we were in the bardic wey
      and fou – lyk hell!

See, poetry is no authentic
no even when ut's near identic
wi dialect – thi warld's no frantic
      tae be a page.
Ye ken why verse is still romantic?
      Ut peys nae wage.

And Burns kent that fu weel – he'd near
ten bairns tae feed, and did his share
o dirt-ferm darg – ye get a rare
      perspective oan
thi poet's art frae a field in Ayr:
      richt thru tae thi bone.

Sae bein English gees you space
tae see ayont thi Selkirk Grace
thi thing that's really in yir face
      aboot wir Bard,
's that high and low brow hae nae place
      in his kail-yard.

Aa leid wiz guid – fae auld Dunbar
tae whit's thocht snash in harsh Stranraer:
whit is thi Scots fur 'motor car'?
      – he'd mak it up:
he wiz bigger than English is by far,
      sae raise yir cup.

leid: language; *fou:* drunk; *darg:* labour.

He wiznae jist some white trash teuchter
a muse seduced while at his pleuchter
tae generate thi genteel lauchter
    o thi middle clesses –
jist as we'd laugh tae hear a tractor
    hud written *Ulysses.*

We use Burns tae promote thi pastoral
and sae we hype him as a wastrel
cause thi thocht's as welcome as cholesterol
    that we're aa creative –
but while we dae nocht he warked *and* mastered all –
    some palliative!

He fermed, he gaithered sangs, he rode
twa hunnert miles a week, he owed,
he trehd tae send thi French a boat
    fuhl o nabbed cannon,
and when he hud thi time, he wrote –
    he knocked his pan in.

Still, why should we admire this form
that's better suitit til thi ferm
and couldna keep rebellion warm
    past Burns's daith,
till fowk think noo ut huz some charm
    and diz nae skaith?

His ram-stam stanza's pell o rhymes
is shairly miles ahind thi times
and whit aboot thi poetic crimes
    his follaers did?
It shid be shown whaur nae sun shines
    and therein hid.

But there's still a merit in collisions
if it's ideas that clash: illusions
aboot oor lives feed oan elisions,
    are friction-free:
but fictions needna be collusions
    o lee wi lee.

skaith: harm; *lee:* lie;

Burns buildit fictive selves frae wurds
thi wey he wrote thi sangs – frae shards
o tunes – nae coorse and common bards
        were really permittit;
he kent he'd be consumed by lords
        and sune oot-shittit.

And sae frae Edinburgh's best
tae Dumfries Toon he wiz dooncast.
Fareweel Clarinda, fausont, chaste
        and no fur probin;
hullo thi barmaid's fouthy breist
        doon at thi Globe Inn.

Tae cope he grew a vocabulair
o selves as weel as wurds – they're there
sae fowk can feel thir heids dae mair
        than hud opinions:
the globe's in there, ranked quair oan quair,
        lyk skins oan ingins.

Thi pastoraulin wee boy blue,
thi Mason and thi drunkelew,
thi rebel and thi preacher too,
        plus four or five,
aa made up Burns's sinkin crew:
        a few survive.

Sae when we batter ancient stanzas'
heids aff thi waas lyk slam-dunk dancers
we micht find that thi action grants us
        a strange sensation;
that fae wir mindset's usual answers
        we've liberation.

And that is why – at least Eh think –
we're gaithert here: no jist tae blink
at fozie kintra Burns, syne shrink
        back tae wir urbane mater,
but tae clink oor glesses and hae a drink
        till a bonny fornicator!

kintra: rural.

Breakfrost

The frost is touching everything before the sun:
each blade has a pencil nudity that makes
the yolk-like orange seem already old,
each flatness reached, brick-like,
as though all cold was urban.
Sheep crunch its windscreen splinters,
horses' heads are glued to it down the blue
flanks of shade. Each leaf is a sucrose flake.
Its intimacy is more exhausting than light.

Morning's sepia, like medieval photographs,
has to fight its way through every scattered grain.
And hollows will persist, like patches left
by the Dark Age bulks of giant sleeping saints,
since Christianity was like a glacier.

Each shadow stuck to it like a tongue
is long and brittle. Everything is biscuit,
feather, spit, viscous, barbed, as though
the land was bait for light, hooking it
and holding it close, gutting the photons
for their kernels of warmth.

The Black Wet

It's raining stair-rods and chairlegs,
it's raining candelabra and microwaves,
it's raining eyesockets.
When the sun shines through the shower
it's raining the hair of Sif,
each strand of which is real gold
(carat unknown).

It's raining jellyfish,
it's raining nuts, bolts and pineal glands,
it's raining a legion of fly noyades,
it's raining marsupials and echnidae,
it's raining anoraks in profusion.
It's siling, it's spittering, it's stotting, it's teeming,
it's pouring, it's snoring, it's plaining, it's Spaining.

People look up, open their mouths momentarily,
and drown.
People look out of windows and say,
'Send it down, David.'
Australians remark, 'Huey's missing the bowl.'
Americans reply, 'Huey, Dewie and Louie
are missing the bowl.'

It is not merely raining,
it's Windering and Thirling, it's Buttering down.
It's raining lakes, it's raining grass-snakes,
it's raining Bala, Baikal, and balalaikas,
it's raining soggy sidewinders and sadder adders.
It's raining flu bugs, Toby jugs and hearth-rugs,
it's raining vanity.

The sky is one vast water-clock
and it's raining seconds, it's raining years:
already you have spent more of your life looking at the rain
that you have sleeping, cooking, shopping and making love.
It's raining fusilli and capeletti,
it's raining mariners and albatrosses,
it's raining iambic pentameters.

Let's take a rain-check:
it's raining houndstooth and pinstripe,
it's raining tweed. This is the tartan of McRain.
This is the best test of the wettest west:
it is not raining locusts – just.
Why rain pests
when you can rain driving tests?

It is raining through the holes in God's string vest.

NOTE: *The black wet* (Scots) – rain as opposed to snow.

A Cockermouth Ballad

(for Michael Barron, and all at Castlegate)

An apple in a garden grew
as big as Magog's head,
then fell, and split in half to show
a maggot's A to Z.

But such a learned maggot in
a medium so gross —
to hint at the completion of
the Legend of the Cross.

Piero Della Francesca in
his frescoes at Arezzo
had only told the half of it
or — in Italian — *mezzo*.

We knew old Adam was interred
with that very apple's seed
beneath his tongue that done him wrong
and thus his skull was treed.

Piero shows us Sheba's queen
pick out this chopped-down beam
for Solomon's new temple as
the rood that had a dream.

Then Christ the warrior climbed up
to Punch and Judy sin,
like Cary Grant on steroids, blow
the Age of Splinters in,

where human seed, the female sex,
all other sects were bad,
but cartloads full of guaranteed
True Cross Wood could be had.

The grey-toothed relics spread abroad
along the pilgrim trails;
were sacrificed to light a witch,
slid under sceptics' nails.

But here and there a seed was snagged
like a pea upon a fork,
and here and there old Adam's tree
bobbed back up like a cork.

In Isaac Newton's garden one
tossed branches at the sky
and one day as he glanced up threw
an apple in his eye.

And thus was gravity first grasped,
a kind of anti-leaven
that stops our mean unworthy selves
from rising up to Heaven.

From A for Adam, C for Christ,
to N for Mister Newton,
the maggot's alphabet was chewed
upon its fruity futon.

But then it curled back to an E
as Einstein set it reeling
by proving space itself was curved
just like an apple peeling.

So History's spelt ACNE, if
you write in tooth and pock;
the future, though, was nibbled in
the script of Mister Spock.

By mind-meld with a maggot, then,
of quite capacious girth
and ample years, I'll try to pen
the last days of the earth.

(Before I do – and let's just hope
that end too is delayed –
I'll briefly mention Cockermouth
where this long song was made

(or on a train near Middlesbrough
to tell the usual truth,
but let that pass) where Wordsworth spent
quite lyrically his youth.

A good home for the ballad, as
Sahara suits the camel,
big apple-gardened Castlegate,
and also William Scammell.

The Derwent and the Cocker clasp
the town in loopy arms
while Southron offcomers prefer
to buy up all the farms.

A fat white spaniel of a man
is statued in its street
embossed with one word – 'MAYO' – as
though that is all they eat.

The council here as everywhere
treat culture as mere tossage;
it's up to Castlegate to keep
art Cumbrian as sausage.

But Michael, Hettie, Chris, hang on,
I must end this dilation,
before my thanks I'll just reveal
our globe's annihilation.)

While the above was being said,
though, back in Cockermouth,
I got too drunk to translate Worm
and then got driven south

through blue half-moonlight smooth as milk
to smoother Loweswater
where in the Barrons' converted barn
I dreamt about my daughter.

I couldn't make the lightswitch work
or find her when she cried,
and yet I knew her absence meant
this darkness was inside.

And then I saw the black-haired girl
I'd known when I was five
play in the pebbles by the lake
and thought 'Is she alive?'

I slapped the switches' tiny eyes
but no bulb came alight,
I heard her walk the corridor
and occupy the night.

And then a bird as grey as slag
that had a finch's beak
jumped on my pillow and began
reproachfully to speak:

'You have a worm inside your head
that's promised to my crop;
you've got its Z, but snore instead
of telling – till you stop

this little girl will plague you with
that hidden gardenscape:
the backies of your childhood – should
you linger or escape?

Was Eden rendered insecure
by something you forgot,
or does your meddling memory
itself pollute the plot?

And is all this a process that
your daughter can avoid,
or must you watch that garden be
repeatedly destroyed?'

I woke to find my mouth had filled
with words as sharp as gravel;
all maledictions on one Zog,
inventor of time-travel.

Although his Company's to blame
for that almighty crime;
to offer to the highest bid
hack surgery on Time.

The churches got a kitty up,
geneticists played ball,
the churches sent our maggot back
to cure us of the Fall.

'Our world,' said Zog, 'is medlar-like;
it rots when it is ripe.'
The worm was stuffed with enzymes that
should change the apple's type.

Since then the worm is in our genes
as peel is in the seed:
abolishing our innocence
is still our only creed.

So Zog improved on lust and greed,
our end's in his beginning:
the origin of sin was just
the wish to banish sinning.

A Heart of Trees

In the big hills of Cumbria
cladded with mist
in that pale green you hate
before Penrith
I thought I saw
a heart of trees,
a cordial plantation
on the side of a hill
bare of leaves
growing through decades.

I'm almost sure
it wasn't planted
in that shape, with that gesture
but I take it as we pass Shap
in this train rushing back
to you, each tree
for a remembered embrace
its branches held up in witness
placing ring after ring
on your fingers.

Whispering Through Ice

My people think it is
in order to talk
with the gods
that I must enter
the frightening place,
and for that reason
fear me and
for fear of that fear
despise me too.
But this is not the case.

When I am there
it is as though
I have been pressed
between two sheets of ice
melting and reforming as
they absorb
the heat of my skin
and innards
until they hold me
perfectly, as
a copper axe is held
within its mould.

From this place I see
distorted figures walking
and talking in the snow,
groaning and
slapping their ribs,
but these are my neighbours
not the gods.
Large as bears
they already inhabit
the frightening place.

My voyage is
the breadth of a fingernail
between
those things they are prepared to see
and those things
on which their eyes
must never fall.
My feet must tread
on a different star
for every step.

For years I only listened
bringing back the news
their own mouths spoke
which their ears
would not hear.
Then I grew distracted
by another people,
another place
glimpsed through cracks
in my ice.
Nothing brought to me before
could compare:
they had grown mountains
in which to live,
surely these
were the dwellings of the gods.

But this was not the case.

The folk there,
although they were
so hard to hear,
these too were my neighbours,
kept from me by time
as my old familiars were
by fear.
They had built years
from their dread
in order to evade
the frightening place.

Held
in my envelope of ice
as a prayer is held
between two palms
I saw how their fear
made time its dwelling:
their past filled
with murder,
they put guilt
into their future.

I prepared
my longest bow,
I gathered up
its double-shafted arrows,
sheathed my sharpest flint
and seized
the precious copper
of my axe
so these people would know
I was a man of power.

I took tinder to feed
my fire, sloe berries for
my belly, and
the mushroom for my mind.
Then I climbed up into
the frightening place.

It welcomed me again:
here
I first learned how
to enter the sphere
where my neighbours' ghosts
wait for
their bodies' acknowledgements,
where
their spirits can
climb out of time.

To reach these others
I must fire
myself like an arrow
falling to the place
no one can disturb
beneath a river
made of ice.

I must wait
until its level falls,
until my lips
can reach their surface
and whisper
what they dare
not hear: only here,
at the point
of greatest fear
can you be free.

Therefore
abandon everything
but what your
terror can teach
and step
within this door,
walk on the sharp
and pointed stars
with me,
and meet your ghost.

Our Lady of the Shells, Our Lady of the Buttons

The coracle takes in water through
its black leathery belly and
saturates his cold behind, but
the red saint doesn't care.
He's slouching with his shins and fore-
arms dangling over
the boat's little hoop, listening to
the monastery bells sound vespers and
ignoring their summons.
He's studying this blueness
of the harebell sky.
He doesn't know this, but
it matches his eyes exactly.
He's contemplating how
to mix this colour for
Our frescoed Lady's latest robe. It is,
he realises, perfect in itself; it is
already the Virgin's robe. He's gazing at
her fringe brushing our globe
as she gazes back, listening to
the prayers of fishermen and fish.
He realises that this sea must be
reflecting the same tone, and sits up,
almost too abruptly, trailing
his untonsured tangle of red hair
like a man-o'-war in the water.
It's never been cut, not since
the moment he found
the Virgin's voice
in his own boyish mouth, not since
he cut himself off.
He leans and tastes the salt;
he licks the oceans for her, as though
his grey tongue was a thread torn loose
from the sky's blue fringe.
He looks down through the waves'
opaque fluencies, picturing
the shining well of women he has painted
on the throat of the chapel

that stood, empty and male,
ten years or so of grey grown through
the red ago. Eve and Sarah,
Ruth and Judith, Bathsheba and Salome,
Elizabeth and Mary, Mary, Mary. He knows
the monks all know
he's not all sane, but protect him all
the same. In his blue cell are
his colour pots and counting bags;
his worldly wealth. In one bag are
orange periwinkles and blue razorshells;
in the other, greatly to the fishermen's annoyance,
are small horn buttons, torn
from their jackets in the first
freshness of the morning, as
they sit and bait their hooks.
He laughs and scoops with
his stained hands until
the coracle spins below the sun,
and sings the bawdiest of their ballads
with the voice of the Mother of God.

The Manuscript of Feathers

Saint and hermit send
each other news by seagull.
They never meet.
They never speak.
They do not discuss
the date of Easter.

Cuthbert on Farne is tempted
by the fur of sea-otters: it is like
the detached pudenda of the mermaids.
The moon is like their breasts:
it presses coldly on the shut balls of his eyes,
it fills their sockets with softness.

Herebericht is safe within his lake,
islanded from demons, speaks
with the freshwater fish about
the scent of home, its wholeness
of moss and quartz.
After this they offer themselves
to the roasting tongue of his cooking stone.

Cuthbert is beset again by gold:
coins of it leap from the evening waters
and cover his raggedy blanket,
every inch chinking with
a drowned king's hoard.
Otters sit outside his hut
and toast him with sunken wine.

Herebericht has visions of apocalypse
in which the world is reduced to islands,
in which the sea is flame,
in which each human sits, naked, sweating, watching
the tide eat at their shorelines.
He sniffs at the pebbles.
They smell jaspery.
They smell of Heaven.

The gull they send between them
carries no messages
scrolled around its leg.
Instead it is itself illuminated:
every feather written on in script
which only they can read.

The Wives of Weinsberg

'I grant the wives of Weinsberg
Permission to go forth,
And each may bear the treasure
She deems of highest worth.
Each woman with her burden
Shall find a peaceful way;
A King the word hath spoken –
The King shall none gainsay!'
DAVID GRANT

It was time to get it over with:
all morning the mocking sharpening,
the concerted whetting of steel,
had circled Weinsberg's walls.
Then the east port was finally opened; so
easy a yielding after long months
of this rough wooing, and,
preceded by their shambling priests,
the women all walked out on war.

At first there came
a simultaneous appraisal. So these,
the besiegers thought, were
the promised conquests, scores on scores
of anticipated rapes, now withheld
by their leader's snatch at chivalry.

So this, the women thought,
is the state of our fields, so patiently tilled,
now ripped up by ballista and wheeled tower,
shat upon for months.
At least the earth would be fertile.

And then the bundles on the women's backs
resolved themselves in the gaining light
into emaciated males, the very men
who'd slopped out piss and oil and stones,
spat arrows till the town ran dry of feathers:
those recognised faces. Conrad's officers had

to run down the lines slapping pikestaffs
with their swords. In his tent
the winner laughed, projecting chronicles,
weighing how much massacre his
fledgeling reputation could take.

At last the command came
to let the procession through.
Hosannas rose, and one girl slipped
her heavy brother to the soil. Instantly
the letter of his order was obeyed
and the supine man was spitted.

Then the harrying began, over yards
and miles, as each woman reached
her limit and let her
lover, father, child, touch
their familiar earth. Only a few
troops were needed, to track
this staggering pack,
handle the amount of fight
the menfolk had left in them.
Some women made it a league,
some made it two; some made it to
the ruins of the neighbouring town.

Then there was one woman, in her forties, with
her one late baby, standing at
the roadside shrine, mumbling, till
she could stand no more; she sank,
keeping the boy upon her lap,
so no limb could reach the ground.
When Conrad heard
how he was lame
he let that infant live.

The Starling Trees

Each evening as I pass the compressed grove
      of trees permitted to flourish on
the university's concrete campus, by
      the Jack Hylton Music Rooms I hear
the starlings shout. At least I think of them
      as starlings, so packed together like
a petshop full of more familiar
      exotica: canaries, lovebirds,
finches and the good to eat, the budgie.

      And I think of it as shouting since
the whole sound has that tempoless constancy:
      an enumerate squirt of cherry stones,
quids of tobacco, a shrill hairdo of noise that could
      be song, percussive as the Bushmen;
clicking like needles, knitting wool concertos,
      recipes of static for the ear
that tries to cook all stations on the short
      wave band into an anthem from

that land of little wings and peanut towers
      from which the cold claws dangle and try
to free Rapunzel's fat one peck at a time.
      It is an event without evenness,
with only evening marking its beginning
      and only sleep its end, though how long
these half-chewed colloquies continue in
      their dreams may not be measured by
the time in which their song persists in mine.

The Baby Poem Industry Poem
(for Robert Crawford)

Sensitive male minus labour pains equals poem.
Production rate increases in inverse proportion
to childcare units as follows:
one couplet per five cloacal nappy non-encounters;
one stanza per non-milky-upchucked-on work shirt;
one poem per missed shift of all-nite colic alert;
one volume per year of missed meals in which
beans must be halved and omelettes rolled
into yellow trumpets, plus three hours
of night-night rituals including
march round marmite-smeared dwelling
chanting 'When-uh sains' and nine renditions
of story about haddock.

Sensitive male supplies plethora of loving
metaphors for partner including:
galactic dugong, pot-noodle of robust abundance,
shining wing-mirror extension for caravans
of completed individuation process,
symphonic Fiorentina team of
graceful scheduling and loving-kindness.
Sensitive male imagines he can see
the creation of the universe
by examining her epesiotomy scars.

Sensitive male's publisher is not impressed,
rendering the sensitive one suddenly aware
of the fact
he has not had sex
for nine months.
He casually but lyrically mentions this
in evening poem faxed home from work.
Sensitive male is suddenly aware on returning home
of unusual ice-pick adorning his forehead.

Partner commences series
of highly-profitable elegies.

Cromag

Reality is being harsh again
in David Craig's old office:
upon a copy of *Marxism Today* for July 1962
with the contents on its cover,
beneath the title 'Satire – The New Revolt?'
and beside the discussion topic 'What is Jazz?'
lies a dead fly on its back with its legs drawn together
like a man's fingers when he's trying to evaluate
something it's hard to reduce
to a quantity.
        It is
a shrewd gesticulation, like
the copse of trees protruding from Millbuies' brim,
that Victorian loch outside Elgin where
I used to walk with Izzie strapped
to my belly, six months old
and being shown the sights I knew
she would not remember.

They'd flooded the valley for
the trout fishers' sake, and now
those trees were leafless digits like the hand
of Daphne, trying to gauge the world she was losing
in the instance of deliverance.

It's like the old word cromag, which
I try to teach my daughter now to use
to mean a pinch of something gathered thus,
between the prints of her fingers –
and I don't know if it will stick
or slip, lie in monumental abandonment
beneath the surface of her idiolect
like a fly with thirty-foot wings
lying on its back beneath the waters of the loch.

The Doll's Tale

Your mind is entering the half-told story
as your daughter falls asleep,
and watching as the doll drops from her hand
into the brimming lake of the drowned volcano,
falling to the boiling stones below.
It looks as though you could reach in for it
and soak your rolled-up sleeve above the elbow,
like retrieving a hairbrush from a too-hot bath.
But that would be to spill everything:
to flood the village where the small girl sleeps,
to make a little lake of the depression where
the doll should lie beside her on the pillow;
to carry everything – cup, plate, cart and chair –
and everyone – the mother who thinks she is awake,
though she is only dreaming this anxiety;
the father snoring, his head awash with other women;
the grandparent in the open coffin
and the girl herself – all carried off without
waking or breaking anything.
Because you do not know where everything ends up
you end the story there, staring into
the pupil of the lake and seeing
the small figure of the doll still lying there
as though she were yourself staring back,
as though that was the price
for not waking up your child, not yet,
to the flood that breaks and batters all before it.

The Giraffe of Urr

(variation on a theme by Selima Hill)

Whilst you still can't speak or read
let me tell you of the time
before you were born
so that this father feels a little
less useless than

the dead tree sticking out
of the dip between fields
seen on the walk into
the Haugh of Urr; the one
which looks like a giraffe.

This is just past the kirk
where that Murray preached
who taught himself more languages
than any other herd-boy
round Anwoth way;

they say the rocks leaked Hebrew
where he used to sit
watching his giraffes
not far from Galloway's
only Pictish carving of a prawn.

In a series of five jars
in this giraffe's long throat
like sisters travelling
in separate carriages
I found these roll-mop messages:

'She will be called the Bald Countess,
she will be called the Onion
Who Must Be Obeyed,
She will be called
My Little Brainstem.'

'She will be a spirit envelope,
a lung tambourine;
she will be a whiney quinie,
a querida,
a primitive tree kangaroo.'

'Her names will include
Darlene Isabella
Paint-spattered Haddock;
her names will include
Fia Maria True Chicken Yoyo.'

'My dear because you cannot speak
I sing for you in the voice
I do not understand:
I know its tones better than
you can ever be known.'

'Confined for seven years
in a giraffe I spoke
words they could not even hear
so powerful is the veil
between your world and ours.'

Grey Thrums

Lissen til
thi baudrins purr
hur grey thrums til
thi bairnie-o;
she's weavan thrums
intil a plaid
tae hap aboot
thi bairnie-o.

She's weavan thrums
o moosewab fur
an feathers fae
green linties-o;
she's weavan thrums
fae mawkies' fuds
an thi doon aff a
yella-yitie-o.

She's weavan thrums
oot o hur dwaums
o claain doon
a hornie ool;
she's weavan thrums
oot o hur dwaums
o grallochin
a cuddie-o.

Sae gin ye dinnae
gang tae sleep
ma pair wee skrauchan
bairnie-o,
she'll weave hur thrums
oot o yir thairms
an hap thum roon
yir thrapple-o.

baudrins: cat; *grey thrums:* purring noise; *hap:* wrap; *moosewab:* cobweb; *green lintie:* greenfinch; *mawkies' fuds:* rabbits' tails; *yella-yitie:* fieldfare; *hornie ool:* horned owl; *grallochin:* eviscerating; *skrauchan:* screaming; *thairms:* intestines; *thrapple:* throat.

Sae lissen til
thi baudrins purr
hur grey thrums til
thi bairnie-o;
she's weavan thrums
intil a plaid
tae hap aboot
thi bairnie-o.

Whilst I Was Asleep

Mute sparrows filled our bedroom
even unto the picture rail
attempting to get in something called
The Spinach Book of Records:
tiny ruthless breasts all
shedding feathers in
a Brownian motion.

The waters of the Moray Firth
shifted
like a restless duvet.

My wife was replaced by a so-so white shark
lying in the bed beside me, its
chinlessness pointing upwards.

My daughter composed her first
Onion Concerto at eight weeks old,
wriggling in her cot.

Pints of sweat deserted me
to rain down on tribes
of desiccated bedmites: flakes
of my skin fell upon them like big mannah.

This redounded to the glory
of some microscopic Moses, whose
place shall be preserved
in the Mattress of the Almighty.

A crow brothel was set up
up my chimney, complete
with cracked mirrors in the brickwork over
sooty silken counterpanes, and over-
priced crow liquor: the sound
of lusty bird gymnastics reaching

even unto Onionland, where
my dreamself was currently reclining

staring only at
a freestanding pair of linoleum trews
(Forbo–Nairn tartan)
containing all the underpants
I've ever worn, each
inside the other down to
my first pair of nappies, all

soiled.

AB Buff

That aa sangs canna be
aboot your nakedness
is meh complaint, no yours,
but there's sma gree or compensation
in kennan aa the blaikers
        in knowing all the challenges to
        a feat of daring
sangs can set themsels
tae get aroond this block.

Some have to pick
the averin at
the back o Balfuff,
        a cloudberry from
        the fictional place,
        Cloudland itsel,
in order to approach
through its taste
yir birkie tongue, tart
        or apirsmart.

Some have to pick
the blue threid fur themsels,
        an indecent touch in a story,
oot o the alasant,
        that striped silk made in Egypt,
in order to escape
thru the hole i the ballant:
        any blank orig-
        inally the singer's excuse
        when his broadside was torn.

Some sangs seem tae muve
neither ee nor bree
but tell blind parables,
        communicate by signs
        in order to conceal
        something from someone present
amid the beust and alshinders,

withered grass and horse parsley,
to find the bilbie o the mind –
a shelter, a liberty wi legs aspar.

Some are that sair hudden doun,
afflicted by the workload
of second-rate fillers for the papers,
the bubbly-jock o Balaam,
that they have to cry
barlafummel, a call for truce
tae the fecht or play.

Some sangs gang tae Buckie
and bottle skate, get lost in
waitin fur the brook o ware,
the deep layer
of seaweed cast up by storms
tae waash up oan the shore,
and the tide tae brime
or fill with salt water
to swell and close the timbers
of their boat.

Some are like you and canna eat
the breid o idleseat;
they must work hard
seekin adminicle, corroborative evidence,
aucht that might help,
are buckers i the faem o wurds,
porpoises atween your A, meh B,
moving towards love at random,
allevolie.

AB buff: the alphabet, so called from the colour of the school primer,
hence something very simple or elementary.

BC

Tyrant, hoplite, Epicurean; all
seemed to live backwards, in

the way I piece my ancestors'
childhoods together, smooth-

ing out their wrinkles like playing
a hairdrier across clingfilmed windows,

planting darker nurseries of hair
and invisibly mending maidenheads.

Thus we all become absurd repairers
of the breaking voices, catchers

of dropping testicles, believers in
backwards film of shattered bowls of fruit

which spring whole from the floorboards
to the trees. Just so the poets unburn

their manuscripts, wipe the soldiers'
excrement from reknitting tatters

of papyrus, and hand their new books to
children who chew gristle like gum:

daughters of the wooden-legged besom,
who gave all but one fur coats;

sons of the millionaire scrappie,
who cast from his palace on the Cleppie

the one who married a Catholic.
Just so their poems can only be read

backwards, beyond their pages
pulping and reprinting themselves

as forests that the letters haunt,
like Pict and crossbill, bear and wolf.

Deep C

Nae buik wi buckskin cover could
contain the case that Eh mak here:
that ilka sang's a city-state,
  each sonnet a Sienna, a Firenze,
  each ballad a Bologna; that it
is larger than the chowk that states ut.
And ilka port's the mirror o uts firth,
  the capital o
uts sea as weel's uts hinterland;
uts river's hert gane dreh
and powrin thru uts streets,
smeekit by the years' reek,
  smoked by its history till
naethin can haud ut that's no cordiform,
  hert-shapit, as big
as a ship or the wame o a whale, as big
as a café, a chip-shop.

Gin Eh could pick oot Dundee's volume whaur
  the pages are aa people and
  the print is chips an fritters
Eh would select the *Deep Sea Restaurant:*
  sae sma a buildin tae
deep fry a galleon in, but ut'll dae
fur thon squid oot o 20,000 leagues ablow
  the dictionary, and
a bar fae Mars.
    Eh'll hae a
fremit hostelry in batter, please,
a Vital Spark tempura, anna
calamari alla Kirk Douglas supper.

Deep Sea, you are the key
tae praise oor toun's persistence in,
as the sea praises gless
by grindin ut wi uts cougherin drone
doon tae a smoky jewellery:
nugget o Dundee, you are a caboshoun,
        a precious stone, polished
        but not cut or facetted;
you are a caduac, an accidental
        gain amang the transitory things.

Deep Sea, you are thi chollers or
        the gills of the Nethergate:
a chuppy i the chappy o the traffic whaur
aa the cauld fish can shoal thegither.

Candavaig an cameral,
cairban and cock-paddle,
colmie an cabelow,
aa's oan show i thon cahute:
        salmon and haddock after spawning,
        basking shark and lumpfish,
        coalfish and young cod.

The canous can clorach in that ship's cabin,
bodach an cailleach lyk a pair o stanes,
        the grey-haired men and women
        clearing their lazy throats like they're ill –
be cantlet up by the caleery,
        bristling at or brightened up by
the frivolous young, the kyaard-tungit,
caller fae thir racy carrants,
        the loose-tongued fresh
        from their rude escapades, still
sticky wi the chalmer glew,
cheekin up tae each ither lyk kissin fish.

And here's the causey saint,
        pleasant as lang as he's no at hame,
chilpy at aa this crouse cantation
        or cold and askance at this
        crude conversation, even though
he's lukein lyk a chowed moose himsel,
        debauched as his wife is calm:
the catfish drink hiz nipped his heid
and gien hur a shiner fur aa hur compone,
lown aneath hur cockernony
wi a chafferon hookit thru hur coat
        sitting there quiet with her hair piled up
        and her brooch bricht by her throat.

And noo we're i the deep end o
meh memory's auld baths, the speak
that the bairnie Eh wiz bubbled up frae,
that wiz owre weet wi hate tae copywattie,
        the exchanges that were too hatefilled for
        a child to remember:
the place whaur faith foond greed
and drink saw pride, and ilk fed oan ither.
Lyk the cauld doors o sunken liners
Eh can see the stoved-in doors o kitchens,
bathrooms cavin in aneath the pressures
that still fill this sunny room.

Whit sang that Lorca nivir heard
can rax intil the deeps o these
auld fish, can reach and live
amang the pressures o their herts?

Scaldfoot

The stumps of the old bridge
                              curve across the river
in a sperm whale smile:
                      krill-swilling, squid-crunching.
I press my ear to that giant acetate,
the bandstand of the Magdalen Green,
that oompahpah omphalos of the known world,
that July when I was ten, back when
McGonagall meant to be funny and
Ossian hadn't made it up yet about the Gaelic.
I'm listening for the tunes they would have hummed
when the bridge went down, if
the bridge hadn't actually gone down,
those creatures in corsets,
those types in toppers –
and maybe it did, the engine I mean,
whistle as it slid through the liquid coal,
to boil the sludge it bothered on the bottom.

With fish in their ribs and weeds through their hats
the passengers still sit, their singing piped
to the well-studded concrete of the stand,
that giant showerhead brimming with hymns.
How hot the concrete gets against your cheek and ear
in the memory's July, how choleric, as though
you were embracing some fever-face,
some slum-girl crushed into the pustular grey,
the tenement porridge that rebuilt Dundee.
How strange the current-coldness of the dead
should seem to blast the ear with so much heat.

My grandmother's father must have known them,
the men who swopped shifts and lived,
or did a fatal favour: he must have known
the space before in which such gestures seem
to lack significance – and did it make
his ear suspicious of such innocence?
We only know he was meticulous in listening
to every psalm his engine knew, each air

it could recite, and that its exhalations were
harmonious beneath his care, so that
he would have understood, in the seconds before
that blaring release that boiled his foot
(which then went septic and drowned out his blood
with hotter poisons), that someone had
broken through our harmonies to where
the corpses sit and hit their keener note
that wipes out melody and tone and breath.

First Fit

Wiz ut Hogmanay or the day afore?
thi fair blarin i thi daurk
an me jist staunin ootside Boots,
whaur thi Overgait yuised tae meet thi Marketgait,
waatchin thi fisses waash past
'Muzik Express' an 'Home's Break Dancer'
stoundin fit tae be
                    thi hertbeat o thi year,
birlin bairns lyk corpuscles roond,
sendin a silent clood
o doos
        tae spirl aboot
                        thi City Square
and push me intae thi present.

Eh'm waatchin white bags waaltz in baldie trees
lyk some marriage atween
snaa an leaves, thi big polythene
foliage o cities. This is me *in situ*,
thi pinball afore thi shot,
wi Lin Yutang's *The Importance of Living*
in an Oxfam bag oan ma wrist,
waatchin thi fisses soom past
as tho ootwith time, observin thi recurrin
wershness o hur mou, again thi slicht
slant o his ee
                as tho these werr
the generaishuns fleein by:

---

first fit: first person to be met or to enter a house on New Year's Day, considered to
bring good (or bad) luck for the year; *stoundin:* pounding; *birlin:* spinning; *spirlin:*
moving in a light, lively way; *soom:* swim; *werchness:* sourness.

that tough wee sockie wi thi stickin-plaistir
aa owre'iz fiss, as tho someone trehd tae peel'um;
thi wee fat man wi a neb lyk a low wattage licht-bulb
an black cat herr thinnin oan'iz pow; thon lass
wi the eyebrows o Nitocris an thi cough o Nicotina –
huv Eh no met thum aa afore, been marriet til thum,
hud thir bairns, intromittit wi them
in bleachin-fields and up thi closes o Coldside,
been uncled-an-auntied by thum, bullied
an brithered by thum, murdirt an touched, up an fur,
money an minny, da i thi daurk, sister still-
boarn i thi dawin, daein fur wan an doin anither –
huv Eh no been swirlin aroon thi swelchie o histry wi
ain and aa o thum, Pict & Pole & Pakistani,
Norman & Gael & Dutcher, Viking & Jew,
Northumbrian & Welsher, Roman leeins
and Armada droonlins, Eskimos oan floes
and Italians in vans: huv Eh no
been ilkane o thum hurryin thi nicht,
buyin burgirs & pehs & pittas & kebabs,
candyfloss & cola i thi cauld?

Naw,

that's a wee bit lyk speirin
is that no Agnes Gardner that beat up Betty Mercer
in Dundee oan November 12th 1521
an hud tae pey'ur fehv shillin?
Or is that that Sandy Paterson wha complained
'certane franschmen clum ower ma zaird dykis
and tane away ma cale' in 1552?
And that fast pair in thi matchin pig-bladder blousons,
ur they no Alexander Clerke and Elesebeth Stevinsone,
banished frae thi toon fur theft and
'gryt sumptuos spending be nygcht continuandly'?
And whit aboot hur in the flooer-print lycra frae Markies,
aye, hur wi thi furst puffy bloom o vodka roond her een,
shairly she's Marjorie Schireham, customar o Dundee
atween 1326 and 1332?

Naw, mebbe no.

sockie: someone walking with an exaggeratedly masculine air; *neb:* nose; *intro-mittit wi:* had sex with; *minny:* mother; swelchie: whirlpool; *leeins:* leavings; *speirin:* asking; *customar:* collector of customs.

There's nae solvendiness tae Dundee's screed;
uts anely alphabet is fisses and
a screel o limbs across thi pehvment's sklate:
a gashlin haund that's got thi shauky trummles,
camshauchle, haurd tae read. Uts historicals's jist
this street and thi fowk scrievat oan ut,
fleerin and fleein lyk pages burnin, ink fadin.
There's nae set text tae net a shoal o,
lyk sparlins fae thi Tay, jist thi constantly
beginnin rebrimmin o a leid,
thi crop o thi waatir, usually crappit in by laddies
or a coo, probably pollutit by a limepit,
not potable, splore-pearls o tint voices.

Tae even sey ye hear ut's tae mak yirsel
MacCaliban insomniac wi stations inniz fillins
that naebody else hiz ever tuned tae;
tae grant yirsel an island atween yir lugs,
a city in a whisky piggie at thi Noarth Pole.
Tae claim ye can translate ut intae script's
tae be thi year's new monstir, mair
cartoon than skrymmorie: a reid herrin-hog, mutatit,
mair like a history minnow, twa-heidit in
print's pollutit Swannie Ponds;
thi recoardin angle tae thi norm,
thi mornin blackie that's hauf-worm, howkin
uts ain tail oot o thi back green o Blackness,
haalin utsel back intae thi yird.

---

solvendiness: trustworthiness; *screed:* a length of script; *screel:* squeal; *sklate:* slate
used for writing on; *gashlin:* distorted, writhing; *shauky trummles:* nervous tremors;
camshauchle: difficult to repeat; *historicals:* historic documents; *scrievat:* written;
fleerin: mocking; *sparlins:* smelt; *leid:* language; *crop o thi waatir:* the first water
taken from a well after midnight of December 31, supposed to bring good luck
for the New Year; *splore-pearls:* drops of saliva ejected by a speaker; *tint:* lost;
whisky piggie: an earthenware container for whisky; *skrymmorie:* terrifying; *reid
hog:* fish wrapped with a red ribbon, a New Year's gift; *yird:* earth.

The Gardener

Ae nicht Eh dreamt ma mither's faither,
that wiz a gairdner til thi Jute Lairds,
cam tae me in thi auld blue dungarees
Eh mind frae thi backies o Corso Street,
and haundit me this buke he hud dug up
amang his roses. He niver spoke, but
Eh kent he'd written ut lang syne
and aa thi script wiz in his haund.

'Eh bide in this gairden wi God alane,
afore Lilith, afore Eve. Eh'm able tae
believe in oor future, but cannae
undirstaund ut. Hoo'm Eh meant tae plaise
ma God or these wimmen wi a lorn
Eh've niver felt, that Eh anely grip
by jalousin uts ruit in God's waant?
Yet sic feelins'll bloom wi sic wimmen
whas comins'll depone aa thi atweens
Eh wull become, tho noo Eh'm primary,
melled wi nocht, and can fiss thon Fiss
nane eftirgangin sall see alehv,
save thon wan unkennin generaishun.
Syne Eh'll be antecestral,
spilet, lang unsainit, till Eh see
Him spelder thi deil's door;
Eh'll be, aa thon burnin while,
thi eildest o skulls. And ma wife,
wha'll dree aa that sae dearly wi me,
is nae mair born than aa hur bairns.
Eh'm owre filled wi virr tae bow an ee:
hoo can Eh be killed? At nicht Eh dander amang
thi green craturs, waatch thir nemms

---

ae: one; *backies:* shared gardens at the back of houses; *lang syne:* long ago; *lorn:* desire; *jalousin:* working out by a process of deduction, imagining; *depone:* set down; *atweens:* inbetween things; *melled:* mingled; *eftergangin:* subsequent; *antecestral:* ancient; *unsainit:* unblessed; *spelder:* split; *dree:* endure; *virr:* vitality; *bow an ee:* go to sleep; *dander:* stroll; *craturs:* creatures.

scell aff them, sciffie aff twigs
tae fins, frae ribs tae rocks. Nemms
are aa ma dwaums, that spraich lyk burds
tae be oot o ma thrapple, that breenge
tae greet thir newous beins, but
can niver grup. Eh waatch them wi
senses Eh sall tine, attention
aa meh children wull loss:
growthe at thi hert o flooers
and braird in thae herts whas dings
Eh'll cheenge when Eh'm dung doon,
gin thon's thi wey ut is. Eh see ut
lyk Lilith, lyk Eve: a fremit thing
that Eh still ken, a haund that's muvein,
weet, afore a yella fire,
branglin me awa intae ma mirks.
Eh strowk thi growins that wull turn
awa; aathin leans in tae me noo
lyk a second sun, waitin oan
anither nemm. Eh ken these wimmen
as plain as Eh can vizzy aa thi lave:
ma bairns as perjink as thi splores
that fuhl thi lift wi faain –
but Eh kenna whaur thir aesomeness
begins: is thon broo brent because
ut's guid, or this jaa strang because
thi man that sets ut sae is strang?
Diz this shilpitness Eh sall betake
oan aa meh dochters, aa meh sons,
depend oan sic distinctions?
God disnae talk, and His starnies'
giddy wheel gees aff paitterns in
a sparple that maks me feel
as seik as Eh'm supposed tae become.

---

scell: spill; *sciffie:* bounce lightly off like a thrown stone skimming the waves;
dwaums: dreams; *spraich:* cry shrilly; *thrapple:* throat; *breenge:* rush; *newous:*
very eager; *tine:* lose; *braird:* green shoots; *dings:* beats; *dung doon:* defeated;
fremit: strange, foreign; *branglin:* throwing into confusion; *mirks:* darknesses;
vizzy: look at, scrutinise; *lave:* remainder; *perjink:* exact, particular; *splores:* drop-
lets; *lift:* sky; *aesomeness:* individuality.

Whit wey can meh anerliness get
sic a fouth? Eh dwaum Eh see
ma ain nemm scrievat in ilka leaf,
ma merk slyte and snoove thi green
that e'en thi noo is shiftin,
findin uts best tint fur thi faa.
Shairly gin Eh clappt haunds noo
baith wimmen wad appear, and ahent them
aa thi croodlin shouthirs o thi warld,
thi ocean's een. Syne Eh'd wale
atween them and this mumbudgitness
that anely Eh brak, that pleys wi
meh wurds as tho they were thi brairds
o uts how-dumbness. Or could Eh choose,
wha kens nae reason noo tae swee
awa frae ony o these unbecomelins?

Eh feel God gowpin through
ma paums, as tho His ain nemm
wiz bein written there, as tho
a cauldrife luke could clean ut
o thi fike that causes cheenge.'

---

sic a fouth: such an abundance; *scrievat:* written; *ilka:* each; *merk:* signature; *slyte:* move easily; *snoove:* glide; *gin:* if; *croodlin shouthirs:* huddled shoulders; *een:* eyes; *wale:* choose; *mumbudgitness:* silence; *how-dumbness:* absolute quiet; *swee awa frae:* avoid; *gowpin:* staring intently; *cauldrife:* chilly, disaffected; *fike:* irritation, trouble.

Hyper

*'I think the future has a way of leaking backwards,
into the present.'*
SADIE PLANT

I'm dreaming again
              of the book that can't
be written even though
              I'm not asleep since
dream texts however
              outré the vellum or
copious the illustrations
              merely alter every time
you thumb through the Whovian stills
              with a white glove
and do not like this book extend
              like a building the
walls and floors of which
              are capable of duplicating
themselves within themselves
              of varying with each
duplication the nature
              of the very model
so that the lift reads

1, 1.1, 1.11, 1.12, 1.13, 1.2, 1.21, 2, 2.01, 2.011, 2.012,

              causing you to reread
the brass company label
              studded in its smoky glass chest
Fibonacci Brothers Ltd
              (some oymoron surely).
When I come to I am running
              a slight temperature
convinced the cover must
              be the hide of Godzilla.

If I could dream this book
                    in a library I'd see
two monks carry it towards me
                    it would be
the illegitimate offspring of
                    the *codex amiatinus*
(the oldest surviving complete
                    Latin Bible in one volume
2060 pages weighing in at
                    75lbs requiring
1550 calves for the parchment) and
                    the *codex cosmographiorum*
mirandi operis (or
                    the book of cosmographies
of wondrous work which
                    St Benedict Biscop gave
to Egfrith of Northumbria
                    for the land on which
Jarrow was founded
                    where the big Bible was made).

There is a northern book-box
                    carved from bone which
announces its origin thus
                    in futhork, 'The fish-
flood lifted the whale's bones
                    onto the mainland. The ocean was
churned up where
                    he floundered on the shingle.'
Something like this might hold
                    our new book's currents.

Its pages flicker and run
                    type size and font alter
words engender antonyms
                    marrowski-isms and slipslops
an illuminated character
                    playing poker in a margin
ends up with a mournival
                    in a hand of gleek
stochastic definitions
                    attach themselves to terms

you'd felt sure you understood
              '*peach:* the so-called spotted cary
of South America, akin
              to the agouti; stump:
commonly beaten with a stick
              before cooking; *salt:*
a low, thick, grotesquely
              contorted member of the goosefoot family...'

This is the guidebook
              to a fluidity that used
to be a city
              and is now your personality.
Bombed and rebuilt in a week
              it remembers everything.
Select your historical period.

In Memoriam Bill Burroughs

'*Every great and original writer…must himself create
the taste by which he is to be relished.*'

WILLIAM WORDSWORTH, Letter to Lady Beaumont

'*…conscience-free, I give true worth.
I sell the best machine on earth.
I'll show you, as well as I can,
Just why I am a Burroughs Man.*'

SALESMAN FOR THE BURROUGHS ADDING MACHINE COMPANY

'*To see another poem about screwed up shit click* here'

Mike Preston's biggest failure in his whole life (Webpage)

Coronation of Bill's Corpse as the Shit-Click King

Dwelling in that imaginary century,
never die where the customary comes first
hard down on warbling World of Wood:
go down on native carpet square knees pleading
Whoop-de-doo Mad Mill Sale OR
Whoop-de-doo Mad Max Miller Sale.
A pint of plain English is your only campaign
the first thick shag of springtime loudly sings
CLICK
Dwelling in that imaginary sanctuary,
a computer reconstruction of a sacked cathedral,
King Shit-Click holds inconstant court.
Guests are offered dainties: denim pasties,
dairy telegraphs, advent colanders, and laminated drizzle.
He campaigns in latex for
I Can't Believe It's Not Food;
his dick thickens subliminally in car adverts;
he voices-over for backwards lagers.
He dwells in aphorisms such as:
'Death: just because you know it's there
doesn't mean it goes away'; and
'Literature is the opposite of cellulite'.
His aphid readers work on through the night
beneath the best humid yak glow
discovering competition entry forms

on the labels of fine wines and
on the bases of ancient pots:
he wins vats of the blushful daily,
customised analects.
He lights his cigars with the gift vouchers
issued by leading department stores.
He tells you in confidence,
'It seems you have an idea
that happiness is vertical
and the last stop is Heaven.'
You have the idea you know what he means
but you realise this cannot be the case.
As you go to bed new clothes keep appearing
on your body: you undress for hours.
You dream of two people and one location:
Themesock, Eighties Max, and St Leonard's Drive.
You have the idea you know what this means.
CLICK
To describe his general appearance in a word
he bears a strong resemblance to Domitian
whose monstrous behaviour left
such a mark upon the Romans
that even when they had carved up his whole body
they had not exhausted their indignation.

Having collected Domitian's flesh
his widow put the pieces together carefully
then she stitched the whole body up
and showed it to the sculptors
asking them to make a bronze portraying
his tragic end.
CLICK
The following morning he asks you anxiously
'Is satisfaction not having any questions?
Did you put ice cubes down the toilet?
Why can't you reciprocate by having a good time?'
Together you tour the palace:
from the Heights of the Fourth Jealousy you descend
to the Garden of the Fifth Meanness.
You jump the haha of the First Envy
and find yourself handed another shopping list:

'Booker guard
changing beef
garlic laundry
drinking crisps
peanut gutter
Hoover-insulting tape'

King Shit-Click proposes a toast

Citizens of Neuralgia, my longing
to communicate with you evaporates
like yoghurt on a spit (initially frozen
as in the key of F) as I look round at
this prestidigitatious sonority
of buttered accountants and meringues of power.
Consanguinity prevents me murdering
your steamed Dictator General (here
cheer) or possibly orotundity or rotundity
as we sit to a static banquet of pigeon
pie and Formica, laptops in filo and roasted
serviettes folded into the napes of swans.
I am pleased as opposed to appalled
(what choice have I?) as I look round at
the personalities of Jerry Lewis and
Micky Rourke frequently
on the same face saying, 'Just keep going,
you'll soon become a classic.'
What choice have I, given the General's
inability to answer diplogastrodic queries like
'Are slugs the slackers of the snail world?
Who licked the spots off this ladybird?
Why does Bored Duck only drink Lemsip? and
are humans the kiwis of the angel world?'
As I look round I am telling you
something I don't want to listen to;
philosophic curiosity as we know it
as we know is as dead as a door.
Nagel has asked [*insert quotation*]
with his arm in a sling in a hat-
box in an anecdote on a bike or possibly
in a bike. *An ekdota*: unpublished things

are us or we, free Coltranes of that
mountainous, transmontane, autonomous and
anonymous nation,
having bought our carnations
from an alsatian
in Central Station;
having drunk the peppery red ink of your
corrective *barszcz*, having coinages
in our pockets which are not
of this realm. We, speaking plurally
and weeping pluvially as Regent
of sheep, not-sheep, and stages between,
of flannel chancellor and channel flâneur,
of minches and munchies; finches,
Crunchies, bunched fingers in the hand
of Baal, of Alba and alopecia. We,
hurrying and hassling, hustling and harrying;
we, growling beneath the imposition
of arbitrary and perhaps
intrinsically meaningless constraints,
we raise our glazes to serrate you!
CLICK
At the court of the Shit-Click King
you're already enthroned, remote
in one hand, penis in the other:
you are Min, the ithyphallic god,
always flanked by two Cos lettuces;
you are Amun, self-fertilising creator of *New Baywatch*.
The Romans knew that lettuce contains laudanum.
Your satellite stations assemble in the night sky.
Your stars buck across the sky
like the eyes of stallions.
You are James Tarbuck, fucking your mother Nut:
who needs blue blood when you've got blue balls?
Red hot and handkerchief, these are your attributes,
these are your salad drips, you are
the non-PC tip, the chief swelling;
you're the bunyip, the tumescent tumour, the Rupert,
you bear the Paul Bunyan of all erectile logarithms;
you're the John Bunyan who fears no global goblins:
this is the Murdoch of all handjobs, you,
you could be king, which means that he

(he being the previous Shit-Click, AKA Ur-Atum,
god of thought and speech
according to the Memphite system,
rider in the Boat of Millions of Episodes,
of *New Crossroads* as broadcast in Kazakhstan),
he must be queen
in the hetero-kerbcrawl-nightcell,
the TV alleyway, the TS I Love You operating theatre,
the jismatic prism that is your subtextuality,
your alpha to beta blocker of a philosophy,
your thick shake with beefcake of big audio diet.
All the king's horses are Triggers with Attitude,
all the king's men are soft white bread.

When shit-clicks collide

Yet again I have to give up
            Yet again I have to grow up
and admit defeat: I am not
            and admit defeat: I am not
in two places at the same time
            in two languages at the same time
(which means that 'and' should be
            ('My nag has a small side' is
an 'or'). Where are these places?
            a palindrome in Polish.)

Can there be 'a mysterious female world
            The runway is marked out
as unlike real life as Star Trek'
            by the ultra-violet of vole toilets.
(I'm already experiencing flashbacks
            Neon signs in an unknown language
from the in-flight magazine) where,
            announce my arrival in the second place.
beside the crashing of the anchovy factory,
            'Elvis's flesh is sweet and tender.'

we watch bee-fighting? 'Reckless said,
            My mug in the cafeteria states,
"I'm going to treat your voice like an egg".'
            'a lamb is shaped like an egg.'

I rehearse again my grasp of foreign
            I purchase it for my daughter, asking
gestures: the thumb, pushed between
            the customar, 'Is this ink potable?'
index and middle, means, 'I don't know.'
            (head on her bosom), 'I must be home.'
CLICK
You are offered free samples of the following products:
Kiwi car forks
toy sauce
tocks
billows
clutter
felt taps.
You realise you have always dwelt within
the shit-clicking court, the mall of malls.
You realise you are living in
the dental cavities of a god.
King Shit-Click offers you
Mrs Ovary's Patented Insurance Soufflé:
it is deep n frothy.
He tells you in the words of Warren Buffet,
'I am a computer.'
You realise you are being wooed, seduced.
You say, 'Who are you if that
is a permitted question with meaning?'
He asks, 'Can we go to a chemist?
I want to buy a cut-out cathedral.'
He tells you he has
a miniature Siamese twin attached to his temple.
He introduces you to the inventor of Permadust.
He offers to sell you
rice bicycles, earth banjos.
He explains, 'I'm not so married now.'
He tells you he has rearranged the weather
so that each hailstone contains
a horoscope or small plastic gift
but you realise this cannot be the case.

He addresses yet another august gathering

Falling asleep in Mothercare
               because Elaine would say things like
I no longer believe
               that people's secrets are
defined and communicable,
               I am proud to be a member
of the League for Protection of Bricks.
               I would like to cut your toenails
in the warmth of my own home.

Greetings to Stang the Fourth
               King of Woodlice, to
Ixat of the Haugh of Un,
               the guy that was the milkman:
Tony Curtis, no, Adam Steele, no
               Adam Thorpe, no, he was Batman.
I serve notice of the right to cancel
               your right to change your mind.
It's all papaya or pomatum to me.
               Your tree is covered in bark.
I have not noticed mustard still
               biting whilst being evacuated
but I sometimes have the curry
               and non-animals like
the mahogany tree.

Idiocy is infinitely
               preferable to guilt, sitting on
a gin-running schooner
               heading for Florida with
milder weather in the South
               is my vantage to exclaim on you
and this of course makes it
               plainly a spirit; it has emerged
from the great tube
               (as long as a cricket pitch)
without loss of identity.

New forms of interiority, more
               reflexive, more negotiated,
remain possible, and with them
               the envelope marked 'Peace'
full of cyanide.

Let us follow the heavy hearse
that bore our old Dream out
            past the white-horned daylight of Love.
Remember: God also said
            let there be Hitler.

They seem to be people without
            any remembered Past
save as it may sometimes come to them
            in the updated pub with perpetual
gas flicker-flame, clutching at
            the authenticity of youth,
the glacier of my fingernail,
            a laugh like a gannet hatchery,
a house that follows like a goat:
            the traces, presumably, of a transformed,
opened-out, but still recognisable
            caravan, a stomach of wrath.
Nor are their feelings full-blown
            and easy to recognise
by the proximity of laughter to death.

I drink and drink
            but nothing disturbs the clarity.
Who can extract
            the cube-root of an ash-tray?
Incrementally, history links up in
            a triumph of the amateur imagination.
I revived deodand
            when I was a boat
and what did I receive?
            Dry Fly Sherry and Scissors Safety Matches,
lard with ginseng and
            a deep-filled lacquer sandwich,
depressed fortune cookies
            ('Few things are as bad
as enthusiastic ignorance')
            chicken fat candles and
the shorts of subsistence farmers.

Dardo can eat
        while we bury him in
a confused sense of having been born
        in some other place at
some vaguely remote period
        at the back of the North Wind
I found Vance the pig crying
        Let thy pale Dead come up
from their furrows of winding sheets
        to mock thy prayers
with what the Days might have been,
        women and chickens first!
CLICK
Having granted that fear of success underlies everything
you have a foundation on which to gather
associated brickwork, such as the distinction between
a politics of gradualism and that
of the incrementalist whose only boldness was
his initial retreat from all democracy
into a blue-walled room where books and pictures
are there to be a clutter on the void,
where nothing keeps the light or darkness out,
where papers, tickets, cuttings, chintzy souvenirs
can only depict through accumulation,
never define singly or protect.
No wonder he is a lazy fellow in the mornings
and never cooks himself a proper breakfast:
'I am always rushing so just have *jyuusu*,
some *pan* and *jyamu*,
with a cup of *hotto kohii*,
while I watch the *nyuusu*
on the *terebi*.'
His girlfriend is an OL and uses a *waapuro*
in her job at a *shinku tanka*.
She sometimes complains of *sekuhara*
when *sarariman* yell *naisu assa*.
She likes *Be-Pal* and *Flash*
and 10% of what she reads is *gairaigo*,
though she does not think this makes her *torendii*.
Her boyfriend explains,
'We are playing you in the adaptation of the century.'
You have the idea you know what he means
but you realise this cannot be the case.

King Shit-Click decrees

'Let one or more persons during a certain period
drop their usual motives for movement or action,
their relations, their work and leisure activities,
and let themselves be drawn
by the attractions of the terrain the encounters they find therein.'
You are aware that he means you.
You find yourself strangely attracted to
his eyebrows or antennae,
to his pubic mouse.
You feel compelled to confess your technical ineptitudes,
you say, 'You know the way that messages are
received from space
late at night on drunken fizzing TV sets?
It happened to me when I tried
recording a whole series
of early Barbara Stanwyck movies.
I couldn't tune the video in,
so I got a tapeful of gogo-dancing molecules.
Then, right at the end,
the point you only reach
after months of overdubs, I saw a face
moving its jaw through the midge-cloud.
It was William in a scene from
Towers Open Fire: who else could
cut across the medium to
mouth his news from everywhere?'
And Shit-Click takes your tiny hand
in his defrosting mouth and grips back
'Mind has multi-
plexes; climb as you will upon
the upland road, until the four-
track craps out, and you get out
and look up at the virus of the stars;
there, upon the silhouetting peaks,
is the twinkling of higher malls.'
CLICK
One in his company late at night declared
that he rose suddenly from the throne
and walked round and round the room.

And Justinian's head momentarily disappeared
while the rest of his body continued
making these circuits.

a second man said that he saw
his face transformed to a shapeless lump of flesh:
neither eyebrows nor eyes were in
their normal position.
Then gradually the face returned
to its usual shape.
CLICK
You switch your radio on and hear Shit-Click say
'a lot of fish defend small churches'.
As you switch it off, the chair becomes a car,
travelling down B-roads of
the infotainment, each convincing you
it is a super-highway.
You see a sign saying 'Warning: seventies aliens ahead'
whereupon
the car becomes a chair again,
and you view
the countryside's B-movies, each
assuring you it's nature in Technicolor,
your very own greatest story
being told and taped by Shit-Click forever.
You hear yourself speaking into the speaker
at a drive-thru decafé. You are saying
'I want a
water-buffalo-chestnut-mozzarella-filter coffee,
I want a'
'And how should you escape the chair's,
the car's arrogance?' King Shit-Click asks, consolingly,
'After all, these sets have been designed for you
to keep on passing through: all's
Wellesian in the world, although opposing
Orson's motto, 'f is for Fake':
you are scoring in the key
of r for Reality.
Dial m here you'll only get
more Motorway: Murder is confined
to the small print of inattention

that will kill you, overtaking on
the brows of days.' The metaphor accelerates,
speeds you through
ageing's villages; it gets you arrested
for winding back the yearometer,
it tries to show you the Keystone Kops
instead of Nastassia Kinski.
But you won't sit for that,
so Shit-Click says, 'Okay,
let's confine things to the apparition of an e
for Eternity, shifting gear
from 'drive' to 'dérive' (that's French, Tish):
simply drift instead of steering, go
wherever the signage suggests.
Let the TV be
a mock turtle swimming in a soup bowl
the size of God's bladder.
Let it be the dream of the dinosaur with
a walnut brain
who woke one fine Jurassic day to find
a tree had grown from its head
and nailed it to the ground.
Let the computer be a cocoon for hatching angels.
Let all the films of Keaton and Wenders unspool
blackly across your mind like
the negative of the white line
still unspooling down a road in God's imagination,
long after the end
of his road movie of the end of the world.
Let all your codes unspool together.'
CLICK
How can you oppose what you have not yet become
while there is still time
phone in your contribution but
please do phone
CLICK

THE MADMEN OF ELGIN

OLLIE (*scornfully*): Do you mean to tell me you don't
know what a myth is?
STAN (*proudly*): I certainly do.
OLLIE: All right then, just what is it?
STAN: A myth is a moth's sister!

   — JOHN McCABE: *The Comedy World of Stan Laurel*

Jacobite's Ladder

Once I dreamt that my head was a stone
shoved beneath a throne in London,
and that a troop of kings and queens
in progressively cleaner regalia
came and sat on my head
for a period of years,
breaking their royal wind into my ear.

As I lay stifled there, I saw
a ladder stretching from the top of the Law Hill
into the soup-flecked clouds,
and climbing up and down this blue ladder
were a series of patriots, some historical,
some fictional: all more real
than the town spluttering beneath them,
at least to the monarchs, who shifted
their faith-defending buttocks
uncomfortably throughout.

There were the renowned Pictish heroes:
Drost of the hundred battles; Brude,
son of Pontius Pilate; and Nechtan,
slayer of mere Northumbrians, all
wearing unknown costumes and recounting
unknowable legends. There were
the triumvirate of television, stage and screen:
Wallace, Bruce and Scottish Play, all
preceded by their faithful definite articles.
There were the terrible Caledonian twins: North
and the Shepherd, Burns and McGonagall,
Louis and Stevenson; and there
were the tribe of Trocchi, all
of whom drank of the waters of Leith and acquired
the power of literary amnesia. That's right:
they didn't know they were born.

Then I was wrestling with Big Tam
dressed as a galley slave
and as we fought he whispered
the history of the golf ball in my other ear:
'Wooden, feathery, Haskell.'
And when he got to gutta-percha
I nutted him with my stony pow,
and as he fell he muttered,
'You'll never get to Marbella
with a shwing like that.'

Then I was the hammer Mjollnir
driving spikes into the blue palms of the sky,
nailing a saltire of jet-trails into place
over Cambuslang. There was writing on
my temples, words cut into the stone,
but I found no one who could read them, nor
could I find a mirror, and yet I knew
these were my land's commandments.
When I awoke, I named the place
where I had rested 'Stonehaven'
and journeyed on my way rejoicing
beneath a great pyramid of cloud.

Farewell to a Stone

Riding out to islands on the little boats,
the open boats of men who would prefer to fish;
riding out to islands with our cameras unfurled,
our children zipped up, clutching our technology
of later; our eyes and hair laughing in
the breeze that we create with money.
We watch the waves go choppy and Byzantine;
we watch the wake blur and choke;
we watch the jellyfish shoal below the brim
in thousands, like the failings of moonlight through
leaves in a soundless forest;
we watch the rims of blackness rise and become

habitable, if not for us then for guillemots:
the pinnacles become multistoreys, a raucous
metropolis of shags and gannets,
the islands socked with puffin burrows like
the bungalows of rural Scots.
If not for them then history, those folk
who didn't need far to walk or drive or shop,
just far to see: the false endlessness of calm;
the sharing of storms, when every rock becomes
your coldest, most Biblical father, ready to shrug
you into the babbling arms of ice
made intimate and fluent, where
your drowned brethren play
football with the heads of seals.

Those folk who occupied the brought stone huddles,
the tiny monasteries and fire-light towers
that seek to stub the progress of horizons
from beyond the sunrise to behind your ribs.
Those folk whose bones they're digging out
as you arrive, the smell of guano and diesel
clinging to your upper lips' grooves,
being thrown onto the unsteady land to look
at thrift and little skeletons, their ends
laid bare in dental traces, shin bone markings;
hopes clutched in pilgrims' shells like beaks.

And then of course there's birds to watch,
toilets to miss, sandwiches to consider:
guacamole dribbling and the egg discolouring
as you observe the jade chip flaring
on the dense evergreen breasts of the shags,
the yellow round their beaks vibrating in the heat;
the silence of a puffin's flight as though filmed
in black and white, the contradicting
Cleopatra make-up of its pincer mouth. A razorbill
drives into the bad end of town.
Guillemots, tail-less, splay their feet out
sideways as they fly, like twin rudders.

Suddenly you've found the cliff's edge isn't
there, but all its drop's in place, the margin between
peering and tumbling fogged
in a curve of tussocks that it's easier to
lie back on, gaze at nothing being various
as clouds and upper clouds and air,
and contemplate the spectrum of emptiness
being crossed by shrieking wings.

And so it is you do not notice
the small stone fall
from your pocket into island grass.
That stone that had started to stand for
your eloquence, that you had to touch
often, for security reasons, that stone is lost.
It will lie among these children of
the seeds that drifted, every blade filled
with the memory of floating; among the bones
of saints who were removed; of islanders
who fed the beacons, and among the birds
to whom all this is urban, ordinary, right.

Port Selda

I remember when all these fields were factories,
when an industry was the limitation beyond which
the city couldn't think. Before
our shorefronts needed to know
what their former yards had built
to fill in the information boards.
This was before the bomb, the bomb,
the modernist bomb,
the bomb that cleanses.

Picture a Heinkel, thrown into a himmelwarp
by passing over Bonnybridge in 1942,
emerging to continue its mission in the mid-
60s and blow Dundee, blow
all your cities backwards.

Wonderfully my grandfather, though dead,
is still on duty in the volunteer fire service,
and able to catch the first few incendiaries,
like women fainting at a dance, vomitting on
their heavy spangly dresses:
his helmet gleams like a pie-dish on the drainer.
But then the heavy-nippled storm begins.
Only the buildings of historic or
architectural interest are struck;
only the quarters of any character are hit.

The bomber is felled by an indignant bottle
cast from Lochee, where its casualties lie,
pants around their smoking ankles,
their budgies gargling their last
in the cracked uncacked-in toilet bowls.
A policeman like a column of oatmeal points
his shaking revolver at
the jute-coloured head of the survivor,
pulled from the harbour, who says,

'The question here is where to put the muzzle?
The stomach beckons, then the ear, the mouth.
Your indecision is built from endings:
it's built of evenings smoking out to sea
in a wake of oil and clocks and bobbing canisters;
it's built of absent records huddled in
your memory's implosive shelter;
it's built of everything that travels back
to the engine – the angel, the heart, the honey.

Through such compelling darknesses
its answer always comes:
' "What is looking for us in all these means?" '

Posada

If there could be a space where I would lose
the need to know things, it would be
the Crown Posada on a Saturday p.m.,
before the scores, while the records are
still turning, churning out their Eckstines
and their Inkspots, their Lenas and Lanzas
and their Peggy Lees.

Green Hindu entrails of the wallpaper,
soft lilies of the light globes,
plaster rhomboids of the roof-beams,
ceiling vermiculations and an entablature
of tobacco gold:
                          none of this drowns out
the sad lads pursuing
a coolness which does not inhere
to afternoon supping: they are
unable to see its
retro serenity. As one old bloke says
'It ought to be in black and white.'

A woman slips off her shoe and puts
her bare foot on the hot pipe
that runs along the base of the wall.
Men as they age discuss
the hernia swell of their hangovers
to something that smothers a day.
Babies who wish to smoke
bring in their mothers.

Mirrors with dark wood frames, with big bosses as though
walnuts could be wrinkled, brain-like breasts,
their glass cut with kinked lines and Victorian ivies;
mirrors lining the wall like windows
project you into that otherless zone
an overhead reflection where
all this is just for you.

That is the elsewhen, the Alice bar, in which
you cannot see the mutterer who wheezes,
Smiler, Eyecatcher, waiting to talk like a dog
waits for crisps. This is the man
who explains one-armed bandits,
who shot at the Mau Mau and got sent home,
who found a baby chopped like brisket.

If there could be a space where I was glass,
sitting at a ghost table, it would be there:
behind the illuminated page of these windows
within the beery book where
a glass stain woman pours
something in a goblet that
a glass stain man raises
to their fruitful tree.

Instead I step back to the afternoon, the leap
of its arch, and the light enlarged by alcohol.

A Breakfast Wreath

Walking down Newgate Street on a Saturday morning
I saw a rasher of fatty bacon lying curled
on the pavement like an ear and thought:

who'd rather have bacon when they could have earholes,
an audience of thousands falling as accidental as snow,
and what if snow is not an accident?

I thought of Mary Trewhitt in St Andrews graveyard
since 1783, on whom all the snow has already fallen:
who'd listen to her smothered story?

Just 45 when Francis the shipbuilder
dropped dead on Christmas Day, and then their son
at 29, and 'Likewise are deposited here

Two Infant Children' of her daughter Jane.
What Novocastrian would stop to hear her?
Even I will not be back: my capacity

to maintain a habit is so poor
as my grandfather's Norwegian guitar knows,
as volumes on the Gaelic and Italian languages mutely
            witness from my shelves;

as the tobacco fields of Virginia,
the tea fields of Darjeeling, the cannabis crops of Morocco
and the barley fields of Moray can all attest.

But for the sake of Vincent Van Pig, whose poor lug lies
on the corner of Newgate and St Andrews Streets
(formerly Darn Close, and I'm sure he thought so too),

and for your sake, Mary, I place
on your grave these metaphoric flowers:
the fried eggs of yellow flags and narcissi,

the sausages of bullrushes and
the black puddings of dark violets,
the bacon rashers of roses and peonies.

Bite on this wreath with your single tooth
as the pavement jaws of Newcastle
chew on the city, and do not haunt me.

After a while we have to go away
carrying the milky, unformed souls
and such nourishment as we are thrown.

We're given so small a role in our dissolution
it surprises us to learn
that it exceeds our personality

as a city exceeds the habits
of its inhabitants. So take the ghost
of that pig and board your husband's ship:

it's been waiting for you these two hundred years,
floating in an ebb-tide of the ears
of the listening dead, and the flowers

of the unlistening living. Sail into the foundations
of everything we try to build on grief,
sail into those stones, and do not haunt me.

Nostalgia for Slush

The light is out to blind us now
there are no more leaves to stand in its way.
It falls through the Durham branches like
numb cut fingers. Thumbing through its cloud thesaurus
it found forty synonyms for pristine,
including *katy-clean-doors, smore-thow* and *wreath*,
but all of them just meant snow.
One cirrus sits in the blue like ski spume
and the melt sheets on the tarmac
like other people's sunglasses.
The cat looks a heavy-smoking yellow.

Nothing comforts the eye but slush
and shade, pacing into each other's greys
in the corrugated print
of other people's shoes. The light
isolates us in our pasts:
the tricks of kick-wading downhill through
rain-pocked and gritty slush,
the lunar feel of it, like low-gravity powder;
the slow forgetfulness of leaky rubber boots,
the smell of socks' incontinence.

I remember the slush of Blackness, of Forthill;
I imagine the granitic slush of Aberdeen,
the small galoshes of Galashiels,
a cut in the wellies of Motherwell:
the white, potato toes
of primary Scotland.

We are dragging those separate seeds of memory,
nearly rendered communal by
the red electric agonies
of returning circulation,
as we shuffle and blink beneath
the undazzled, dazzling gulls
to which all this looks like
another waste of waters.

Lament for Burt Lancaster

I must have been swimming in my sleep again,
the way you crossed America, that narcoleptic continent,
diving in pool after waveless pool, always
the same pool, always the same
bed I wake up in, knotted in the weeds
of my locked muscles, drowned among
the accreted remains of words,
to hear that you are dead.

Surely some piratical sheet could still be cut
to send you sailing into the rigging
and evade that extra's plywood cutlass.
Surely some cranky bewigged professor could
have capsized your drifting iron boat
so that you sank to the blue beneath
with a torpedo of air to breathe,
and simply walked ashore, blindly,
a lobster in manacles.
Couldn't you have attached hooks to your noose,
and only seem to be hanged, as in
that wannabe-medieval Lombardian piazza?
Surely there was some nondescript door
that opened back on the fifties in
a burnished spume of cigarette smoke,
a bulbous envelope of cadillac,
that could slip you away in monochrome.
Surely you could have simply strode,
Kirk Douglas at your dusty side,
down to the noon-bright corral
where everything is always OK
except for the Clantons.

You, who chewed up the gristly toads of producers,
even their spatulate dollar-green feet,
without betraying the slow dignity
of a prince of Sicily. You, a showman, whose hands
could bear that great torso's weight up
a pole, elevate you to the tower's top.

When did you first suspect that bearded, mute,
brightly-toothed companion, Nick Cravat,
of being Death himself, following you
from trapeze to screen, catching you always, then
attaching himself to your unslippery heels,
and seeming to vanish. Only you knew
he played your shadow in part after part,
embracing you in the premonitory flicker of screen deaths,
preserving you for this. the stroke and the slow
decline, screenless, lineless.

Couldn't you have gone by screaming train,
Kirk envious as always by your side,
crashing through the border into
Mexico, desert, beyond,
surrounded by the stunned and unsuspecting angels,
full of kicks and punches still? No,
you were most truly the birdman by
the end, hand patting your lover's withered
cheek like a wing, letting
go into the heart attack, climbing beyond
our memories' cameras, releasing into the filmy layer
between dignities, between identities,
above princes and marshals, beyond angels.

Czech Cartoon Poem

Everything is drawn
in long browny
pastel crayon lines

which swirl and un-
knot before
our swiftly moving eye

into a field of folk
buried in neat rows
up to their waists.

Their arms are buried too
and their long hair is tied
into a topknot.

Males face females, but
everyone watches the sun
move slowly down.

a current of deep red
washes over them, then blue,
then they close their eyes.

We enter the nearest
man's head: flickering,
a cottage interior.

Children tumble before
a fire, a woman cooks
broth. Looking

into the pot
we see bobbing lumps
we recognise as

the man's head, smiling
and roughly-chopped.
We're thrown out as

he screams silently,
staring at the face
of the woman opposite.

We enter her head:
there are a number
of tumours.

These are shaped like
swedes, like grand
pianos, and like fish.

They are swelling rapidly,
and only one
will dominate.

A tuna fish wins, leaving
desiccated turnips,
withered keyboards.

It seems to be dawn:
a yellow head appears,
then yellow shoulders.

A yellow giant strides
across the field.
The folk clatter

their brown teeth.
He pulls up the men
and throws them in a heap.

They have no legs,
just a mass of white
and tangled roots.

Tears roll from
the man's head
whose dreams we saw:

each one contains
a naked child who runs,
dripping, to the woman.

She opens her mouth
and they jump in.
Through her eyes we see

them swimming from
a large fish
with gaping jaws.

Remote

Hoo'dye get haud o
thon hot wee remote
that contrasts ma feelins
fae 'hate ye' tae 'dote',
an colours ma fizzog
fae blae tae beet-reid
by turnin thi volume up
inside ma heid?

Dye ken that ut turns oan
thi screen o ma breist
sae you can hae sicht o
whit programme's oan neist?
Gin yir no keen oan
Dundonian soap,
flick tae thi sitcom
Fummil & Grope.

Check oot thi info
oan meh teletext
tae find oot hoo heichly
or laichly Eh'm sexed.
Scroll up thi previews
fur whit's 'Comin Sune':
ut micht stert at midnicht
or this efternune.

Erase aa thi tapes
that dinna pass muster
based oan thi wooins
o Wisdom and Buster,
but save me wan Capra
or Eh'll truly ken
hoo bitter thi tea is
o General Yen.

blae: lividly pale; *beet-reid:* beetroot-red; *neist:* next; *heichly, laichly:* highly,
lowly; *shougle:* nudge gently.

Wan thing alane
ut cannae adjust:
meh TV aerial's
angle an thrust;
say an thi pikchur's
no juist as ye waant
ye'll hae tae cam ower
an shougle uts slant.

To a Mousse

O queen o sludge, maist royal mousse,
yir minions bear ye ben thi hoose,
O quakin sheikess, lavish, loose,
        dessert o fable:
ye pit thi bumps back oan ma goose
        and shauk ma table.

Ye lang cloacal loch o choc,
grecht flabby door at which Eh knock,
and wi ma spunie seek a lock
        tae mak ye gape,
ye flattened, tockless cuckoo clock
        that drives me ape.

Come let me lift ye tae ma mooth
and pree yir pertness wi ma tooth –
ye slake ma hunger and ma drouth
        wi wan sma bite:
come pang ma toomness tae thi outh
        wi broon delight.

Let ane and aa dig in thir spades
and cerve oot chocolate esplanades,
and raise thir umber serenades
        at ilka sip:
sweet Venus, queen o cocoa glades
        and thi muddied lip!

pang: stuff; *toomness:* emptiness; *outh:* utmost.

Chopsticks

You arrive like two legs slid
into a single paper stocking:
kneeless, *à pointe,* joined at your bamboo hip,
half a person awaiting
the awareness of fingers,
the mirrorball of an open mouth before
you can dance on the rice-strewn floor
of an emptying bowl.

You are drug-stuck lovers
joined at the heads,
you are goalposts with a foreshortened bar,
you are a gate through which
a bone-thin password must be whispered
before we can enter the garden of good appetite.

Your snap as I part you
is sharp as a shot,
is the opposite of a gnash,
is the wishbone of a geometric chicken.
It is the sound of one stomach clapping:
it announces the breaking of all fasts,
the beginning of all feasts.

Gin

(on Kipling's 'If' winning the BBC poll on National Poetry Day for the nation's favourite poem, forever)

> *'...we must not confuse the intensity of the poetic experience in adolescence with the intense experience of poetry.'*
>
> T.S. ELIOT, **The Use of Poetry & The Use of Criticism**

Gin you can drink a bottle of gin
    and not puke up in the Garrick;
gin your leg got caught in a bear-trap
    at Gordonstoun whilst sneaking back
    from the Duffus Arms, but
    you bit it off and crawled
    into your dorm;
gin you can wipe out millions on the Stock Exchange
    because you failed your Arithmetic GCE;
gin you can grin and take it whilst
    a half-cooked lobster snips
    your knackers off at Cowes;
gin you can snort a greenie on the plebs
    from a private box at Covent 'Lottery' Garden;
gin your wife can wear a hat
    with a peak of lacquered horse entrails
    into the Royal Enclosure at Ascot;
gin you can argue that riding to hounds
    is the only humane way to keep down
    the population of hunt saboteurs;
gin you can push a strawberry up
    a school governor's arse with your nose
    at the Henley Regatta, whilst keeping
    a Roger Moore eyebrow raised, and thus
    get your boy into Ampleforth...

Gin none of the above actually happened except
　　　　in a Horlicks hallucination during
　　　　Keeping up Appearances;
gin you listen to Richard Baker's dozen but
　　　　detested Paul Gambaccini; bought
　　　　Delia's recipes but wouldn't actually
　　　　cook her meals; didn't notice during
　　　　Nick Ross's heated phone-ins on devolution
　　　　that no one at once Scottish *and*
　　　　north of the border
　　　　ever bothers to take part;
gin you can keep on claiming to be Home Counties
　　　　while all around you are frantically
　　　　digging up half-cousins of their granny's
　　　　that were Welsh, or just trying
　　　　to become Irish by osmotic consumption
　　　　of Guinness and Muldoon;
gin you can't remember a single poem written in
　　　　the last fifty years because
　　　　the ones you think you like
　　　　scunnered you so much at school
　　　　you don't read any poetry anyway –
pick up the phone and back
　　　　an exceedingly good versicle
　　　　for you alone
　　　　are qualified to vote.

NOTE: 'Gin' (hard g) is Scots for 'if'.

History of Sock

Sock is sold at
M & S slave block attached
at ankle to Siamese Sibling.
Owner frees Sock
with tender snip
of plastic connective tissue.

Sock is an inveterate something
without a bra, or
Sock is not an invertebrate, but
Sock is no sad sack, rather
full of shapeless hopes.
Sock regards Foot
as a parasite.

Sock is navy blue with
lycra and cotton content to
easily grasp Owner's
concept of war against taste.
Sock empathises with Owner's
restraint of irrational opinion;
Sock is a logical being.

Sock does not speak to
Sibling, whether
in drawer, basket or
revolving bin of deluge.
Sibling, on the other foot, regales
Sock with unlikely tales
of their common coal and bogcotton origins.
Sibling has
creative limpings.

Sock disdains creativity, sport
and sneakers, releasing heady
pungencies as defence.
Sock disdains lawn-treading
and weeding duties:
Sock is not a piece
of garden hosiery.

Sock is lost in soiled condition,
somewhere between Saturday
laundrette and
rented flat.
Dog in Voltairean mode
pisses on Sock.

Sock regards overnight stars
as possible subspecies of the cufflink.
Sock remembers being pulled on
to Owner's hand
to be rolled over Sibling
in neat bundle. And
vice versa.

Further Dog in dog mode
sniffs and then pisses on Sock.

Owner having retraced sockless steps
locates Sock. Owner is appalled at
Sock's bladder control.
Sock is reunited with Sibling
to whom Sock does not speak:
Sibling limp-ankled poet, whereas
Sock has now seen Life.

Letterbomb

Too late: by the time you have read this far
your right hand is metaphorically waving to you from
the ceiling saying, 'Farewell: now
you understand what it is to be *car-cleughit*
as the little hand of Scotland feels,
moving slowly from hour to hour of its history
while the big hand of England birls
through moment after thrilling moment!'
And indeed all the mirror-glass frontage of your mind
has just blown away, placing icy fragments
in the hearts of Kays the length and breadth
of the Home Counties, turning them into
MacKays, and you are looking North
for the first time, noticing two women
being drowned by dragoons in Wigtown Bay
on 11th May, 1685, for refusing to take the Oath
of Abjuration. You are unsure what they
are meant to be abjuring. You notice
for the first time the continuous public protest
throughout Scotland from 3rd October 1706
to 16 January 1707, during the final debate
on the Treaty of Union; and the conspicuous
movements of English troops at that time
to the Borders. You always had the impression
there was a referendum, or it was good for trade,
but this is now hanging by a flap
of metaphysical tissue. 'Help ma boab!
I'm bein lectured to oan Anglo-Scottish relations!'
you think, then: 'Crivvens! I'm thinkin
in Scots!' This is because the letterbomb
has blown away your Great Vowel Change,
and the noisome gap it leaves in your palate
is emitting all these ridiculous Scottish noises:
hirdum-dirdum, keiltch, catch-match, femmel, tory-worm.

No longer will you alight at Waverley for
the Festival thinking, 'Do they talk like that
when I'm not there?' Or raise a weary eye from
the first line of a 'Lallans' poem saying
'I simply cannot understand this stuff; it's like...'
(without actually being) '...a foreign language.'
'Goad help us!' you exclaim, realising
the disintegration into pseudo-dental fragments
of your cultural sneer means you are actually
shedding a tear over such terrible clichés as
the systematic butchery of Highlanders in
the wake of Culloden, and the huddled clans
shuffling aboard ships during the Clearances
which you are now aware continued into
this century. 'Whit can this mean?' you enquire,
as volume after volume of contemporary Irish poetry
spontaneously combusts on your shelves,
perhaps in sympathy, and behind them you notice,
for the first time, volume after volume
of contemporary Scottish poetry.
'Yet this is anely aestheticism, eftir aa.
There is nae real boamb, jist as the Scots
waant nae real independence, there is anely
the idea o a boamb, typical o that abstrack naishun.
Thir hurts are aa centuries back,
and lang since covert by the guilty bandage
o complicity in colonialism; therefore
ma hurts are equally illusory, ma wounds...'
At this point the loss of blood to your argument
causes you to fall, the first victim of
the Scottish Informationist Front, and their note
crumples in your fingers: 'Free yourself first.'

car-cleughit: left-handed; birl: spin; hirdum-dirdum: confusion, noisy mirth;
keiltch: to jog with the elbow, or heave a burden further up one's back; catch-
match: a match of great advantage to one side; femmel: to select the best, dis-
carding the remainder as refuse; tory-worm: a slug ('tory' is a term of contempt
and dislike, applied to a disreputable, deceitful or tyrannical person).

Free London Now!

We think that you can make it on your own,
we're damn sure that you're big enough to try.
Just order your necessities by phone:
our scooter fleet delivers by and by.

The latest lettuces can be imported,
the literature, of course, was never yours:
your publishers may well be feeling thwarted,
we'd still like back our inky little hures.

We agree that industry is not your problem,
and ditto with our strange infected meats.
Send back our homeless thousands and we'll hobble them,
so at least they won't clog up your golden streets.

> *We want our alkie shouters back*
> *and our despairing Dans:*
> *we'll just restock the Highlands with*
> *a slathering of the clans.*

Our Festival will move beside the Thames
to save expenses for those still at college.
You'll be our little Hong Kong of the Names
where everyone who stays must have the Knowledge.

You'll have a lovely round of leftish chatter
and all the theatre this life could want:
to lose provincial towns that bathe in batter?
Small fry if it dislands a debutant.

Forget that single Scottish correspondent,
no more reporting 'blah-rain-blah-chill' weather:
we'll try to all be brave and not despondent
at least we're all non-Londoners together.

> *And what about the rest of us?*
> *It's nice of you to ask-o*
> *but you never were the sunshine source*
> *in which we liked to bask-o.*

It's bye bye Geordies, Scousers, Mancs and Brummies,
Ta ta to Taffies and the Cornish too:
but a bit of Belfast is forever Mummy's
and we think the Falklands will abide with you.

Of course the lack of cricket will be awkward –
at least in Oz the Ashes are at peace.
As for the London Irish: send them Knock-ward.
The London Royals? Germany and Greece.

So that's the Empire finally dismantled,
you never thought you'd see it in your *Times*.
Each Trouser-leg of State is now well-ankled,
and each Miss Brodie-talking shop is primed...

> *Hold on: the London vote's just in*
> *or is that rather 'innit'?*
> *They've voted that they'll have us back!*
> *(Though not on* Just a Minute.*)*
> *Our Outer Vote is rendered void*
> *and Vera's singing like a linnet:*
> *But what about our bulgy sack*
> *of prayers all wrapped in Disunion Jack?*
> *Oh that! Who cares? Just bin it.*

No Joy

Black didn't know the difference between
Gaelic and Scots, not even when you told him,
but it was his bookshop we were reading in,
so we didn't. First his girlfriend sang some old
   keens, samey-sounding heart-stop things,
     then we gave the usual session: all-in flytings,

works outings from Hell. Now she was Irish, so
you might have thought he could be curious
what she was singing in his face, but no.

What she was saying, after, when the four
or five of us went drinking, me and Black,
Wedderburn, and some poet from Missouri,
was: 'You Scots have no joy. Where is the fackin
   joy?' Well I looked beneath my plate but found none.
     'Where,' she orated, ' 's the joy?' chewing that fond noun.

She was getting felt up by him and drunk
quite suddenly. I thought about the Irish
girls in my family, the Torberts, who shrank
away from poverty to meet the dire
   marmalade lodges of Dundee, and got
     a nest of Protestant boys all thrown out

of their fond fathers' miserable wills.
I thought about them in the lip-reading mills,

their one gins at their proper Hogmanays,
their snorting snuff and swallowing small moothies,
their litanies upon each other's dying days.
I checked out Wedderburn declaiming truths
   like a Wee Free – how Burns was some humdinger –
     to a drunk girl sitting on another man's finger.

Marshalling time again for the cranial mince.

I checked my Harris tweed jacket for joy,
I checked my Donegal overcoat, since
it was a cold night for a northern boy
in the metropolis. I took my brains
    to Brasenose to check my English pockets,
        since some Scots come equipped with multi-sockets.

She told me all the way to the last tube
about joy, while I searched the white hairs on
her boyfriend's head for traces of the substance.
Perhaps the freckles on his hand would join
    up and spell it out. Surely this, if any
        hand, should be pleased, to touch both her and money.

Wedderburn meanwhile was far from his partner
(whose name it was) and weans, examining
the tonsils of the drab American bard for
flecks of pure joy with his fine rauchle tongue.
    'This creature,' I enquired, 'where were you going
        when you saw it last and just what was it doing?'

The Madmen of Elgin

Recitativo 1

Thi time Eh bideit in thi Laich,
thon bonny brimmin fousome quaich
    o furthy barleycorn,
Eh'd cairt ma bairn lyk a papoose
jist up thi hill ahent thi hoose
    each fairish simmer morn,
tae pint oot tae a six-month-auld
    wha heard but couldna say
thae touns that lig atween thi fauld
    o Findhorn and thi Spey:
      that bairn wiz starin
        at somethin primary,
      she joukit and lukeit
        at somethin mair nor me.

And ilka nicht that Eh drove doon
thi Linkwood road and intae toon
    past thi distillery,
Eh'd see thi daurk wiz fuhl o hocus
thi wey she'd luke withoot a focus
    oan ivry hill and tree.
But Elgin's sae hoaked owre wi fumes
    that mebbe caused this gliskie:
uts Chanry Kirk's aa awald tombs,
    uts deid aa drunk oan whisky.
      Decayin and swayin
        they canna jist bide still
      thi pair deid huv sair heids –
        ut gars ye hae a swill.

---

fousome: over-rich; *furthy:* hospitable; *lig:* lie; *joukit:* bobbed; *ilka:* each; *hoaked owre:* covered over; *gliskie:* glimpse; *awald:* overturned, like a sheep lying on its back and unable to rise.

Song of a Stranger in the Ionic Bar

Eh jist came in here fur thi bathroom
Eh jist came here tae use thi loo;
Eh don't waant tae speak to nae fuckers
and therr's no way Eh'm talkin tae you.

Eh jist came in here fur a swally
and mebbe a double or two;
Eh don't waant tae breed wi your collie
or interface now with your shoe.

Meh nostrils do not waant expandin,
meh dick disnae need a tattoo –
Eh'm as shair that yir girlfriend's a stottir,
as yir colon's shair it's a kazoo.

The time has come when Eh must leave ye,
Yir acquaintance Eh shall not renew;
Eh'm jist aff tae cuckold and thieve ye
while you sit in here and yahoo.

Recitativo 2

Ootfrae thi bar some young dudes went
        wi Bells and Irn-Bru:
aneath thi auld cathedral's tent
        thi faithless nicht air blew
and aa thi ghaists o Elgin leant
        thigither at thi grue:
thir anely hame a hattered shent
        whaur Casuals went tae screw.

swally: swallow; *stottir:* stunner; *grue:* horror; *hattered shent:* ruined, vandalised disgrace.

Song of the Sub-Welshian

When A wiz jist a little cunt
ma mither geed me a fuckin dunt
wi a fehv irin
richt oan ma skull
sae A jist laid me doon:
she wiz a punk on junk
she smelt lyk a langdeid skunk,
ma daddy wiz jist a drunk
nae tather abaa.

    (*Chorus of Casuals*):
    Nae tather abaa abaa
    O say huv you seen wir baa
    we kicked it richt through yir waa
    nae tather abaa.

When A supported Hibs fur kicks
ma fuckin freends were totally pricks
we shat oan auld wifies
fur livin too near
tae Gorgie Road's surroonds:
as lang as it soonds lik Hell
ye ken it will sell and sell
fur Londoners like thi smell
of a wee bit of rough.

    (*Chorus*):
    A wee bit of rough's enough
    tae pairt you fae valued stuff
    tae protest is to get duffed
    by a wee bit of rough.

When A wiz Casual as ye please
A geed thi lassies ma knobby cheese
they sais 'Caa that shaggin?
Take better aim
and don't use the hole that's broon':
hoo lang diz thi Buckfast last?
Hoo fast is a speedfreak's past?
And noo A've assembilt ma cast
nae tather abaa.

(*Chorus*):
Nae tather abaa abaa
O say can ye see yir baas
we kicked them richt ower that waa
nae tather abaa.

Noo A huv needles of ma ain
and track mark tattoos richt doon ma banes
though E maks me haver
and ravin's inane
A jist write aathin doon:
in a windmill in Amsterdam
A smoke thi pot o thi bam
A'm cream-o-thi-crap-o-grams
A yam whit A yam.

(*Chorus*):
We yam whit we yam we yam
we think he's King of Siam
wur heids ur filled up wi spam
we yam whut we yam,
whit's Hibee's Hibee
whit's Hibee's Hibee
whit's Hibee's Hibee!

Recitativo 3

Inben a hoosie owre thi waa
        chowkfu o china, broon wi photies,
a bachelor wiz caain awa
        his een a mess o flecks and moties.
His sister hud gote free o'ur duties
        tae him by deein, sae, by himsel,
owre fuhl o fear tae mind auld beauties,
        he sat – at his ingle, in his smell.

inben: within; *chowkfu*: packed; *caain awa*: just keeping going; *een*: eyes.

NOTE: Heart of Midlothian's ground, Tynecastle, is on the Gorgie Road, Edinburgh.

Song of the Mizzle-shankit Man

Eh beek ma fire sae braw
but canna keep thi cauld awa,
it anely gees this chill
the stour-look o a stervin will.

Thi thing Eh feed, Eh'm shair,
is fear that ootwardness waants mair
when things that arena sae
hae nae need tae be bauld or blae.

Hoo human is ma rule:
a flameless bleeze needs orra fuel,
ingyre thi hope o heat
and dinna tak extinction neat.

When cauld and daurk descend
whit ither ingle dae you tend?

Recitativo 4

Thi furst o speerits, chief o ghaisties
rose up noo, his fiss aa pasty:
this wiz John Shanks, wha ton by ton
hud cleared thi stanes frae haily grun
when Elgin's kirk wiz slap and slaury
fur whilk he's crehd thi Bishop o Moray.
He goaved at sloth, at hurdies gaen
and lat oot this maist scunnert maen:

Independence Blues

So ye were born in New Cumnock
and went tae thi skail
and learnt hoo tae parse and talk proper,
there wiz Burns and his spider
and Bruce wi thi moose
and Watt thi inventor of porridge,
and ye played fur thi Rangers
each playtime or plunked
but wid ye no like tae be Scottish?

146

So ye went tae thi college
tho yir parents were puir
and yir best freends aa cleaned fur thi Cooncil,
there wiz apeshit Monboddo
and auld Burke and Hume
and MacDiarmid that lived in a cottage,
and ye learnt that oor learnin
wiz pure sceptical
but wid ye no like tae be Scottish?

So ye warked in thi Borders
in a sma legal firm
and mairriet a maik hailed fae Melrose,
there wiz bairns and thi Ridins
and rugby and bools
there wiz agein if ready or not-ish,
there wiz one thing not proven
in all of yir deeds
sic: wid ye no like tae be Scottish?

So ye early-retireit
and bocht a wee croft
and tried tae dig peats and speak Gaelic,
there wiz Duncan Ban Dorain
Big Moog o thi Sangs
and midges tae nip at yir dotage,
and ye bagged aa thi islands
yir yacht could swing by
but wid ye no like tae be Scottish?

So ye voted 'Yes Yes' when
Sean Connery asked
like thae lassies that geed in tae Bondage,
there wiz Pussy McFlora
and Folly-a-Bloom
and Jean Mon Armour of the Forest,
and yir parliament sang
'So we anely live twice'
but wid ye no like tae be Scottish?

mizzle-shankit: having legs spotted by sitting too near to a fire; *beek:* to feed a fire; *stour-look:* stern appearance; *bauld or blae:* vigorous or sickly; *orra:* ordinary; *ingyre:* presume upon; *ingle:* fireplace; *slap:* gap in a wall; *slaury:* a mess; *goaved:* stared appalled or stupidly; *hurdies gaen:* backsides going (copulating); *scunnert maen:* disgusted moan; *plunked:* played truant; *maik:* partner (in marriage).

So ye died and were buried
richt next tae yir dug
and went tae thi place God expectit,
there wiz Knox and his trumpet
and plenty Wee Frees
and MacKellar Watt's meatiest sausage,
but Saint Andrew strolled over
and said 'are ye dead
or could ye instead jist be Scottish?'

Recitativo 5

Blin Jamie neist cam feelin hence
thon poxy thief wha, mim and mense,
could cut a suit or sclim a fense
    wha, frae thi jile,
aince crept tae nab thi evidence
    and spile his trial.

He could recite auld Milton's dite
oan Adam's slump and Satan's slyte
o tongue. He sat apairt that night
    and felt thi mune
upon his lids lang rowed in shite
    and hummed this tune.

Song of the Ghost of the Thief

Ma brithers aa lig safe frae hairm
but canna find thir lassies' airms
ablow thi causies, undir fairms
        they whistle fur a claut o thum.

    (Chorus)
    Ah am a thievan, reivan man
    tae tak yir purse wiz aa ma plan,
    thi richest poke that met ma haund
    wiz whistle fur a claut o'ut.

Ma brithers niver foond a joab
whaur maisters didnae daily rob
thum o thi gowd and laive a boab –
    they whistlet at thi claut o'ut.
    (*Chorus*)

Ma brithers went tae mony a war,
thi Empire splairged them near and faur
and blaudit thir wits intil thi glaur
    they whistlet fur a claut o thum.
    (*Chorus*)

Thinicht thi madmen aa sall rise
and sit wi fowk that still hae eyes
and ask fur oor immortal prize
    we'll whistle fur a claut o'ut.
    (*Chorus*)

Recitativo 6

This sang sent aa thi lassies aff
    relieved tae rin hame screamin
as bodies brust frae gress and graff
    lyk Michael Jackson dreamin.
Thi stupit laddies stood aroond
    lyk stookies, lang and stith,
Eh coontit up the corses, foond
    thi livin werr inwith.

Tam Watson telt hoo aa his fleet
    wiz dockin faur inland,
Thi Garb wiz fiddlin i thi street,
    Mad Russell luked deid grand.
Feel Clarkie snuffed speed up his hoot,
    Feel Robbie louped owre cars,
Mad Innes gaithert us aboot
    tae talk o lust and stars.

---

mim: quiet; *mense:* sensible; *dite:* piece of writing (here *Paradise Lost*); *slyte:* an easy, smooth motion; *rowed:* wrapped, covered; *claut:* touch, clutch; *poke:* pouch; *splairged:* spilled messily; *blaudit:* dashed; *glaur:* sticky mud; *graff:* grave; *inwith:* less than another amount.

A farewell to fucking

Ladettes wi pricks fur pets
wives wha dae thir duty,
those wi dugs lyk Buddha's lugs,
drained o hope and beauty:
thi female division departit tae Mars,
left us tae pin-ups and broken-doon cars.
Rubber money, black fish,
eat football, drink pish.

Smarter Marthas
wha dae it wi each ither,
lust-manx wha jist can't
because thir cunt's their mither:
thi she-shaped gender migratit tae Venus,
omittin tae pack thi dysfunctional penis
Rubber money, black fish,
eat football, drink pish.

Thi mithers of aa yir battlin bairns
have gone tae thi mune tae kick doon thi cairns
yir booncin boys hud raised up there,
tae lig by thi seas
and brush dust frae thir hair:
they've taen thir mousses, thir sunscreens, thir gels,
and left you thi bratpack, uts snot and uts smells.

Thi weemen, thi weemen are Mercury-boond,
sae wha's left tae stroke yir slavery hoond?
Rubber money, black fish,
eat football, drink pish.

We spend oor daily wombless wad
on stilettos and eyeliner,
fulfil thi weird of Auld King Cod,
'Each man his ain vagina.'

---

buckies: whelks, seashells and snail shells generally; *ankerstock:* a large long loaf,
usually of rye bread; *loons:* young men; *rammish:* crazy, uncontrolled; *siccar:* sure;
gane green: rotted; *doolie yetts:* ghost-haunted or graveyard gates; *weird:* fate,
often laid upon one by magical forces.

Recitativo 7

Thi ither madmen croodit fast
    aroond the livin's heat:
George Edward's mairched his Toon Drum past
    and kept tae thir hert-beat;
James Calder beat thi Egyptian ass
    that still trod on his feet;
Mad Chalmer's hair wiz still a mass
    o buckies, croons and peat
        that swawed that nicht.

Mad Innes wrote a letter to
    'The Door-Posts o thi Toon',
Mad Russell yelpit 'Gardyloo!'
    and spun his gowd waatch roon,
Tam at his ankerstock did chew
    and knocked aa lurchirs doon,
and Jamie offert tae lassoo
    thi lassies frae thi mune
        and raird that nicht.

Thi loons began tae offer tae
    thi madmen swigs o liquor,
some rammish weemen reared fae clay
    and gar'd thum oaffur'ut quicker:
gee Nonny baccy and ye may –
    or not, Eh'm no jist siccar;
see Eppie Moonlight and ye'll play
    this tune gin you're a vicar
        aa sang that nicht.

Song of the Madmen of Elgin

Consider yirsel gane green
consider yirsel ane o thi baney-band,
Daith's growein in you sae deep
ut's sure you're waatrin um in yir sleep.
Consider yirsel wurm meal
consider yirsel gane thru thi doolie yetts:
there isnae a lot we tak
and Mac
there isna nae comin back.

Gin ut shid faa fur us that we shid lust tae loss a snood
we'd hae tae toss wir shrood awa
mebbe thi fact that we are stiffs wirsel
wid stey wir dobs
then a-dirlin loons let's cwa!
Consider yirsel intestate:
ye'll niver nae mair feel greed,
fur eftir you've been six-fut doon and tint yir pate
consider yirsel fairly deid.

Consider yirsel gane gyte
consider yirsel ane o the loony tunes
ye're mangit in mind and rave
you sump, you're numptier nor thi lave.
Consider yirsel a gowk
consider yirsel clocked by a cannonball:
ut's anely thi glib that talk,
hey Jock,
ut's better tae glaik an glock.
Blahblahblahblahblahblah!
Naebody trehs tae be behaviourist or Freudian
cause we'll moider them wi dool
anely ut's wise tae caa canny wi thi doiter-dorts
when there's doctors you must fool.
Consider yirsel insane:
ye'll no be aa that far aff,
fur eftir you've been roond thi bend and back again
tae consider ocht else wad be daft.

loss a snood: lose someone's virginity or fornicate in the open air; *stey wir dobs:* stiffen our members; *a-dirlin:* a-screwing; *tint yir pate:* lose your head or skull; *gyte:* mad; *mangit:* deranged; *sump:* simpleton; *numptier:* stupider; *lave:* the rest; *gowk:* fool; *glaik:* stare stupidly; *glock:* make a stupid noise in one's throat; *dool:* misery; *caa canny:* be careful; *doiter-dorts:* states of depression; *chittert:* shivered; *snashin:* insolent; *dottlet:* crazed, uncertain; *slypes:* heavy, flat-footed steps; *spavined:* walking as though spavined (a bony excrescence or hard swelling on the inside of the hock of a horse); *daffs:* foolish or vulgar behaviour; *lirk:* wrinkle; *crousy:* brisk, bold, cheerful, comfortable, proud; *nichts and nochts:* darknesses and nothings.

Recitativo 8

Sae raird them aa, thi ruined waas
shook and chittert lyk tae faa
        and bat and houlet flappit;
they stauchert aff wi snashin laughs,
wi dottlet slypes and spavined daffs
        that Eh alane still clappit.
And Eh alane in Elgin's kirk
    consider hoo thi land
hauds deid and livin in wan lirk
        upon uts crousy hand,
                and grinning, begin then
                    ma final fling o chorus:
                this aff-cast loonie's saft last tune is
                    Izzie's and Deborah's.

Song of the Drunken Husband

Meh bairn she thinks sic wickit thochts
she disnae ken ur bad,
hur brain is fuhl o nichts and nochts
that ken na hoo they're glad.

Meh wife she disnae luve thi fuil
wha thinks she is sae fine:
she luves thi man Eh cuid be and
thi lad Eh wiz langsyne.

Meh country canna be utsel
fur sicht o whit ut's no:
a rose can niver ken uts smell,
wir deeds tell weal frae woe.

Tae blinly dae fur luve's thi thing,
thi anely lane Eh'll pint
till aa thi deid begin tae sing
and warlds click oot o jint.

Beppe

'I believed in the cupid
I thought I'd kiss you for all my life
I guess I'm just a little stupid
now I'm going back to Rome'
FRANK BLACK

Signori, man whose name confirms his status,
Giuseppe – Joseph – player without fuss,
a footballer who's filled with that afflatus
that English footballers can just discuss,
but Italy's as full of as a plate is
of verdure from a region stuffed with suss
and savour: Lazio, a name that seems
best fitted to the better of Rome's teams.

(At this point half my audience just got restive –
most women cannot stand this sort of sport:
they read it as so boring it's suggestive
of men adoring men – and these deport
themselves in acts so violent, yet festive:
it's foreign as a legionary fort.
But let me, since my whole theme needs defending,
explain it tends to stray before its ending.)

Legs and the ball I praise, admittedly,
but also our affair with what we've lost:
the places, people, goals that pass away
unvisited, not loved enough, or tossed,
like suspect salads, out; the things we say
'I know that now' about, and mean the cost.
And what has this to do with well-kicked bladders,
or snakes with apples, stockings, venom, ladders?

Well, it was black-lunged Italy that got
me smoking at nineteen with all those cheap
delectable packs – the tobacco a shot
of shredded autumn bootlace, but this sheep?
That shrugging style was what I thought I'd bought:
Nazionale: join us – just breathe deep.
Fifteen years on the tempting tongue extends
to meat: inhale a deli – eat your friends.

Sometimes I feel that other life's so close,
you know: the one we've always spent in Rome,
from when we never broke up, or your prose
became worth millions, and could transfer home
to a flat that's almost up the *al fresco* nose
of James *Gazzetta* Richardson, the foam
on his cool capuccino covering where
you sit while he reports and dry your hair.

I could report how clean – neck-breaking shiny –
our tiled floor is, or how we never changed
the electric orange curtains, or how tiny
the hip-bath is, popliteal, deranged.
Then there's my saint liqueurs, a sweetened briny
filled with drowned plastic martyrs: drunk, estranged.
I won't discuss your pant display, or say
how our waistlines faced all that confectionery.

Perspective just prevents my being able
to identify the colour of that hair
and name the 'you' in this suburban fable,
and so I must return to that fine player,
Signori, interviewed at this same table,
still *capocanoniere*, in the glare
of winter light and that fanatic eye
tifosi turn on, meaning 'Score or die'.

And here those unfamiliar with the lingo
may also try to leave this poem's stadium,
thinking this sounds like stuff sung by Domingo,
just further proof that football equals tedium.
But say they mean 'top scorer', 'fans' and bingo:
you start to know why Beppe's my Palladium
(the statue that kept Troy a while from swords,
Rome being Troy's new town) – to whit, the words.

There's something in all slang like making love:
cant's full of it, and even jargon's juicy.
There's something in a match's kick and shove:
that grappling with the earth that's black and bruisy.
Your team's a pair of hands, the net's a glove
you can't all fit – and football's none too choosy:
the one who scores becomes that extra digit
that stills all language's delighted fidget

into one cry: you interrupt it if
you must with Freudian guff – like how each team
gets pressed into the ground, how it might have
its back line penetrated – why not claim
ecstatics don't require some big hot stiff?
All words abase themselves before this scream:
all creatures know that others want their pleasure,
and only those who lack it attack leisure.

So why not raise a glass of white so blond
it catches like his beard, his hunch of hair
as he swoops down on passes, eels beyond
the heavy red of Roma's backs: he'll dare
a shot that skims across the keeper's pond
and makes him seems all frog. And let me cheer
his dance above the all-embracing dirt
and praise the very colour of his shirt.

(Though let's have something northern in that glass:
Lazio's *bianco*'s got some of Gepetto's
shavings in it: it's rough as Nedved's pass-
ing or those streets where we are not well-met
till lightened of our lire. *Veritas*
demands we knock back wine that's *del Veneto*.
My palate won't be guilty of such fibs,
like old Pinocch, or pseudo-fans of Hibs.

And that's another stand of audience
who've started shuffling for the exits:
those whose obsession with football's a stance
defensively picked up from books – don't mix it
with me, a Dundee boy kens well the wince
of doom, kens Jim Maclean could never fix it.
I hadn't dared to watch a game for years
till Lazio awoke those good old fears.)

It's neither sky nor sea – too pastel, more
the blue tone of those little swimming pools
they build beside their villas, tempting for
the would-be Anglo-Tuscan, he who drools
for all Italia but must just explore
the emptied wallet common to such fools.
That wily paleness is the colour of
the shirt he wore for Zeman and for Zoff

– and Erickson, but now my story spins,
becomes Shakespearean, gains Terentian slants,
with the exchanging of two *Calcio* twins.
For from Sampdoria Erickson transplants
Mancini, fifteen years the furious prince
of Genoa, marcher from the field in tant-
rums, back-heel master, forward whose huge grace
means only he could take Signori's place.

This Aztec cut left Samp without a soul
and Lazio with forwards by the yard –
the six-yard box, that is, where, boot and jowl,
they wheeled, bobbed and collided till the hard
law of *Fortuna* meant another's goal
gave Beppe's captaincy the reddest card:
embarrassed squirming on the has-been's bench
with just his buttocks and his teeth to clench.

Hard cheese, as hard as Pecorino, when
we know that scorer, Per-Luigi, was
about to be dropped or transferred, and then
secured the only goal that rates applause
at Lazio: the one that means a win
against those Roma dribblers-without-cause.
It hardly matters, but he also scored
that goal against the Russians – but you're bored

again, and let that irony go out
of play. So would it help to know that Gigi
(that's Per-Luigi Casaraghi)'s pout
and shanks are famed by girls from here to Fiji?
('Brindisi' 's better but the rhyme sticks out).
No – no point pointing out that goal's the squeegee
that wiped the sweating TVs of a nation
clear of true nightmare: World Cup degradation,

for my result's the same – Signori's years
of glory ignored by you and Erickson.
Dear reader, why don't you pop out for furs
(unfake, alas) in Milan; catch the sun
(unscreened, preferably) – disdain my tears,
go crown yourself King Semiotic's son
in fat Bologna: leave me to lament
the downfall of my hope's last monument.

I love the way he lost, laconically
handing back three goal leads, as though the like
of Lazio don't need defensive play.
I love the way he took one step to strike
so no one could predict a penalty.
I love the way he would refuse to hike,
but just mooched round that frantic moshing box
then scored, or held up games to adjust his socks.

In short I see I loved my would-be self –
in shorts, and poured in an Italian mould –
but still my kind of idiot, neither Guelph
nor Ghibelline, not really, but controlled
by one huge need: be loved or hit the shelf;
excel but never show – and don't be sold.
It drives you like a duty if in common
with Beppe you can recognise this daemon.

Be loved, not be admired or famous, be
the one who's held to hold the game together,
not even by their conscious mind, but see
the way the team, your family, all tether
themselves to you, or gather in your lee
as though you sheltered them from ugly weather,
like something without failings they could know:
what could he do on losing this but go?

And here's the strangest twist of the stiletto
for who should need him more just then than Samp?
Still mourning their Mancini's allegretto –
that galvaniser of the park whose ramp-
ant glance itself could kick balls through the net-o.
And so you flew north, to ease Sampdoria's cramp.
Heart-swopping stuff, though neither of you clicked,
both being footballs fate herself has kicked.

So, goal-less in Genoa, has your art
deserted you? How does the *bella* game
look now, Ovidian Beppe, forced apart
from Nesta and Gottardi, not one name
you know to slide that nutmeg you could dart
behind defenders to convert and tame:
the ball a pagan only you have blessed,
a comet being shown its proper nest.

Bereft of Boksic, tragic in attack,
for one whole season by your twisting side,
tall and direct where you seemed small and slack,
but while you struck his every kick went wide –
he did the same at Juve till, bought back,
he hit a sudden match of shot and stride,
and now, when you are gone, his every week's
a fusion of his chutzpah and technique.

And last there's Per-Luigi, never *dux*
while Boksic and Mancini are on form,
but still the stealer at that breathless crux
of goals that push your old team from the swarm
in which Sampdoria flounders. There's no *pax
romana* that can heal your parting from
a striking partner so insightful that
you seemed to land on four feet like one cat.

And now Favalli's led them to a cup
the lees of which you must drink every night:
it is the case that other men pick up
those trophies that we once assumed we might;
they live in places where we thought to stop,
but now can see propelled us on a flight
without a destination we would name,
so we say '*Ave* failure, *vale* fame'.

I'm like that with Catholicism, stuck
upon the only Protestant outcrop
the Herberts made in fifty years of fuck-
ing anything confirmed. And now that Pop's
sneaked off to Donegal, rejoined the Flock
of Flocks, it's on the Proddy rocks I stop –
except supporting Lazio makes Rome
a place of worship, sacred to this poem.

Except you're gone, Signori, leaving me
as usual in between those moving posts
like that time the train stopped at Empoli
returning to Firenze. At the most
we'd half an hour to stroll – no time to see
more than a darkened street. We were two ghosts
haunting a place we'd never lived, but knew
as wordlessly as dead things do:

we read the menus we would never eat
and window-shopped for goods that stayed unpaid-
for: great gelatinous hot chocolate,
sketch-pads for our next visit – never made.
We looked into the closing bar whose set
was turned to some then crucial match that played
out to our uncommitted eyes till when
the hooter went: we left that town, those men.